# LEAD ON!

# LEAD ON!

## A PRACTICAL APPROACH TO LEADERSHIP

Rear Admiral Dave Oliver, Jr., USN

PRESIDIO

The views expressed in this book are those of the author and do not reflect the official policy or position of the U. S. Navy, the Department of Defense, or the federal government.

Published by Presidio Press
505 B San Marin Dr., Suite 300
Novato, CA 94945-1340

**Library of Congress Cataloging-in-Publication Data**

Oliver, Dave, 1941-
    Lead on! : a practical approach to leadership / Dave Oliver, Jr.
    p.   cm.
    ISBN 0-89141-427-4
    1 . Command of troops.  2. Leadership.  3. United States. Navy-
Management. 4. Oliver, Dave, 1941-  . I. Title.
    VB203.075 1992
    359.3'3041—dc20               91-34664
                                      CIP

Typography by ProImage
Printed in the United States of America

*With thanks to the individuals who provided my early leadership—Dave and Dorotha Oliver of Indianapolis, Indiana (formerly), and now Fort Myers, Florida; and Walt and Nondus Bithell of Blackfoot, Idaho.*

# CONTENTS

# PREFACE

I was inordinately fortunate during my early professional career. I worked for some truly awful leaders.

Thus, during the subsequent free time that life sometimes provides, I always had a full wagonload of professional grist waiting to grind. The important questions were always the same. Why had my bosses acted without apparent thought? Why didn't my supervisors understand the effects their actions had on people?

Why had our team always done everything the hard way?

I have spent hours on these questions.

It appears that leadership principles are applicable across a wide spectrum of human endeavor, and I hate for the winds of time to quickly scour away what I so painfully learned. I thus have written down some of the situations I ran into during my climb up the career ladder and what exactly I took home from those experiences. You may disagree about the particular nuts I choose to pick for my knapsack. If a friend also reads this book, one story or another may even lead to an argument. Good. Important ideas deserve emotion.

And whatever else leadership is, it is important—to us as well as to our society. If I have learned one thing in my first thirty working years, it is that leadership, just like Mother's washday detergent, is at least a double-duty ingredient. Leadership first makes individual efforts better. Then leadership melds the individuals into superior teams. Leadership is the modern gunslinger that walks into town, throws the bad guys out, and then stands astride the county line, ready for trouble, arms akimbo at his sides.

Good leadership is that inexpensive multiplier for which everyone is searching. If you aspire to be a leader—if you think you are a leader—you are the person I want to reach. Please take my torch.

I can't make the normal disclaimer that the stories herein don't represent real people and events. On the contrary, they certainly do. Because some of the events happened some time ago, one or two of the facts may have been altered inadvertently. If you know better, sorry, it is the best I can recall. On the other hand, the dialogue is deliberately constructed—I heard something like what is quoted.

I witnessed each event; in some I participated. I have been deliberately inexact about my particular stool at the bar. Specifying my role wouldn't add much.

You are going to find a great deal of discussion of nuclear submarines here. I hope you are not put off by what may well be an unfamiliar environment. I think I have included enough explanation that you will learn something about what is involved in submarining as well as the difference between good and bad leadership. This book is definitely not just for submariners. However, I spent much of my early life building, repairing, or operating submarines, and those experiences often clearly demonstrate a particular point critical to a story. Subsequent to those early years I have worked with aviators, surface warriors, special forces, Air Force and Army men as well as women,* politicians—even civilians! I believe the observations in this book apply not only to all of those people but also to each and everyone of you who is trying or intends to try to lead or manage someone.

There are also several examples in these chapters describing how Adm. Hyman G. Rickover handled one issue or another. (Admiral Rickover is widely credited with being the principal architect of the nuclear Navy, and often received equally broad criticism for his personal leadership style). I have inserted some of my personal experiences with Admiral Rickover into a story when it seemed pertinent. You will have to draw your own conclusions as to whether I approved of his style. Whatever you decide, if you then ever meet someone who worked for or with the "kindly old gentleman," you will be armed to carry on one heck of an argument.

If, when you finish this book, you want to check the pedigree of any of the lessons that may have taken a liking to you and followed you home, the last chapter is a summary of what I meant to say.

---

*I am a gender-neutral author. *He* and *him* should be read as *he/she* and *him/her*. *Man* can often be read as *man or woman*.

# CHAPTER ONE

## Patience

A certain number of readers should skip this chapter. It doesn't matter that it is early in the book. There are lots of other good chapters later. You can pick up the central concept then. If I mention any specific gems, I'll be sure and summarize them in the final chapter. Your personal health is important. If injustice gives you a headache, or if your stomach churns when the bad guys win, you will probably be much better off just to pass this chapter by.

This is not a pretty story.

So warned. . . .

Once upon a time, in one of our fleets, all of the ships and submarines and most of the airplanes were dispatched to search for a three-star admiral who had reportedly gone down with all hands aboard one of our nuclear submarines. Everyone who could possibly help was scrambled to look for survivors.

Now let me tell you up front that the good part of this story will turn out to be that no submarine had actually been sunk, and in fact the admiral was right then fast asleep, in the best bunk aboard the submarine, dreaming the dreams of the just (all admirals dream such dreams).

Unfortunately, there was a bad part as well. The bad part was that all of the Navy had been officially told that the admiral, as well as the submarine in which he was sleeping, were lost. So when the admiral woke up, he was going to be very, very embarrassed. In addition, every sailor on the coast had been called out of his home, and warm bed, and back to his submarine, ship, or airplane to look for this admiral and his submarine. When this effort turned out to be un-necessary, all of the sailors were also going to be very unhappy.

What actually happened? Funny you should ask. To recreate the scene we first need to go back in time a few more hours and visual-ize ourselves at sea, down beneath the blue waves, aboard a subma-rine. Imagine. Are you there yet? Good. Find your way to the control room. Right, the one with the periscopes. Ask any one of the crew members. They are used to new people aboard being confused. When you get to Control, stand back out of the way and watch. There—over by the radar is a good place. Now, remember, this incident occurred several years ago. This was before satellites made communications to and from submarines so much easier. At the time of the story subma-rines had a great deal of difficulty talking with anyone—especially with each other. Given the options available, many submarines rou-tinely communicated with each other by means of what was called an underwater telephone.

If you have never talked on an underwater telephone, it is similar to talking to Hong Kong on one of those cheap telephones you get for answering an advertisement for a magazine. In the water sound travels along an anything-but-straight line, bouncing off fish, slowed by kelp, bending with changes in temperature and salt content, and arriving at your ear as only a ragged shadow of its former self. This tortuous route is not the only path each sound wave can take, and the same words often arrive later as faint wavering echoes after bounc-ing off the surface of the water or the rocks on the bottom of the ocean. The delayed echoes add to the garble of an already almost unrecog-nizable voice.

Some days are good. It is as if the speaker were right at your ear. However, on most days the speaker could be on Mars trying to yell direct, and you would get roughly the same information.

There were, and are, all sorts of ways to help get around these problems. You search the ship for someone who can enunciate clearly. You use words with lots of consonants and make the message abso-lutely as short as possible. No "whereases" or "therefores" here. You break even short messages up into parts, and pass them a sentence or two at a time. You s-p-e-l-l. You speak slowly. You project your voice lower. You ban anyone who has even driven through the Bronx from ever touching the microphone. Got the picture? People get better with practice, but it is never easy to communicate with the underwater telephone.

So, there we were that day, our submarine acting as the bad guy, and the other submarine filling the good-guy role. The three-star admiral was on the other ship.* The training we were doing required us to meet the other submarine periodically at specified points in the ocean to restart the problem. For some reason I do not recall, the other ship decided to change the geometry for the next phase of the exercise. So they pulled up beside us underwater and directed us to stand by to receive a three-part underwater telephone message.

Okay. The officer of the deck pulled out a pen and notepad and stood by to copy. He picked up the underwater telephone handset and reported that he was ready. The other ship passed the first part of the message. The officer of the deck carefully listened and wrote down each word he heard. Two other officers, passing by, heard the incoming transmission and realized that communications were going to be difficult today. They also grabbed pieces of paper, took positions close by the loudspeaker, began listening intently, and started writing. So far, so good.

Helping out in deciphering underwater telephone conversations is standard procedure. Some people hear higher frequencies with great fidelity. Other people hear low frequencies well. As the frequency of the human voice is often drastically altered while going through water, you don't know if a word is going to come in with a high or low pitch, or even if you are going to hear all of the syllables. When a message is coming in, everyone writes down what he hears. When the transmission is over they compare notes.

That's what normally happens.

In this case, the commanding officer was a very impatient man. He was also very sensitive to the image he presented to his seniors.

The commanding officer knew that the three-star admiral (his boss's boss's boss) was on the other ship. The commanding officer knew that if the admiral were in the vicinity of the control room of the other ship he could hear their replies. So, when the transmission was over, ("Whiskey Papa, this is Oscar Sierra, stand by for message in three parts. Break. This is part one. Break. Intend to alter tiepoint for next event, over.") and the officer of the deck looked over at the other two

---

* In the submarine force the admirals and other senior officers routinely ride different submarines for a day or two to determine how things are going down on the deck plates. This was one of those routine trips for the admiral.

officers and said, "What did you guys get?" The commanding officer snatched the handset away from the young officer and spoke clearly into it: "Oscar Sierra, this is Whiskey Papa, roger part one, over."

Now Oscar Sierra and Whiskey Papa are code names. It isn't important that you know how we determine or use them, but it's the way we do it, and it gives the message a little authentic rhythm, so I left them in. They obviously stand for them and us. In that order.

The next word in the message is key. "Roger" means "I have heard and understood." So "Roger part one" meant that the commanding officer was telling the other ship we had heard and understood what they had sent in the first part of the message. The "over" meant that he was through talking, and that the other ship could transmit some more without stepping on our lines.

Then, after the commanding officer had sent that message in a very clear, articulate, distinct voice, which probably sounded very commanding when broadcast from the loudspeaker in the control room of the other ship, he took the handset away from his mouth (he did not hand the microphone back to the officer of the deck), and said to his officers, "What did you guys get?"

And the three officers, who had compared notes by this time, showed him what they agreed part one of the message had said.

Meanwhile, the commanding officer's "roger" and "over" had travelled to the other ship at about 823 yards per second, and the other ship had begun transmitting part two, which gave us the time for the next event and the latitude of the new rendezvous point. And the instant the "over" from the other ship warbled into our control room from its perilous journey through the water, the commanding officer brought the underwater telephone handset back up to his lips and said, "This is Whiskey Papa, roger part two, over," in what was also a very deep, measured, commanding voice. Then he turned to his officers and said, "I didn't quite get all that, did you?"

The latter, who were scurrying as best they could, showed him what they each had, and he nodded his approval. So far it looked as though they had understood every word.

Now both submarines were still moving while they were talking. So they were passing into and through water with different characteristics, different numbers of fish, and different amounts of salt. And submarines at sea are always moving relative to each other. One may be slowly moving up toward the bow of the other, from where he is easier to hear, or, alternatively, sliding back toward the stern, from which it is not so easy. So there are any number of reasons why acoustic conditions change, even during a relatively short conversation. In fact, change is the only constant at sea.

When the third part of the three-part message came over, the commanding officer, as before, acknowledged by saying, "This is Whiskey Papa, roger, out."

The "out" simply means that the transmission is over. Now it certainly would have been better if the commanding officer had said something like "roger, wait," which means exactly what you think it does—"hold it for a minute, I'm thinking." Or, on the other hand, if he only hadn't said anything until he knew that one of his officers had actually heard the message, that also would have been okay. But, as we have already noted, he was an impatient man, and above all he wanted to appear commanding and decisive. So, since we were supposed to have gotten all the message, then we must have.

"Out" says "we've got it."

And then the commanding officer put the handset down and turned to his officers and asked what the third part of the message had said.

Unfortunately, none of them had quite heard it.

Double unfortunately, when the commanding officer frantically picked up the handset and tried to raise the other submarine, our opponents had already turned away and beat feet. They were nowhere to be found.

Triple unfortunately, without knowing the exact longitude, there are quite a few possible meeting places along the thirty-six thousand miles of one particular ocean latitude.

Etcetera unfortunately, the instructions for the exercise specified that if either ship did not have contact with the other for a certain number of hours, then the first submarine should report the other as missing.

We didn't know where they were. We couldn't find them. Ergo, they must be lost. After the required number of hours, we reported that status and then surfaced to take charge and coordinate the rescue operation.

It got a little more absurd, but more won't help the point. Within a day the situation was unsnarled and the airplanes and ships were permitted to return to their home ports. I'll come back and tell the rest after some digression about leadership.

Leading people is a fascinating profession. It captures our attention in much the same way a professional baseball game does—

because those who truly understand the game realize that even the most elementary play, performed at the professional level, is much more difficult than it appears.

Leadership is the same. Practiced at the professional level needed aboard submarines, leadership is both subtle and difficult.

Have you ever watched one team or ship or group succeed again and again, while others never do? That is the tip of the leadership iceberg. The best leaders truly have the ability to take theirs and beat yours. And then trade, and take yours and beat theirs. Is it any wonder that the subject of leadership has such fascination for anyone who works with people?

Now I maintain that one of the most important characteristics of a good leader is that he is alert and sensitive to the thoughts and feelings of the people working with him. The good leader, whether or not he shows or is even aware of his own attentiveness, constantly senses the emotions and thoughts of his people. He knows even before the individuals do which emotional chemicals are at this moment coursing through their bodies.

The good leader does not necessarily change his goal based on the emotions of the moment or day, but he adjusts what is being done to harmonize and harness, not only the total physical and mental effort of the group, but also the group's thoughts and emotions.

The exceptional leader does this without having to think about it.

I do not know whether one can learn to be a great leader. Some men and women lead so effortlessly that it seems implausible that leadership is wholly a learned skill. But I do truly hope that it can be learned, and I know leadership can be improved.

And I do know this about a good leader. A good leader is patient.

This is not to say that a good leader always refrains from letting a particular failure result in an "emotional experience" when there is something *particularly important* you want someone to never, never forget. I even believe, for the very, very critical issues, the sight of the leader figuratively cutting someone's throat in public can serve to define, much better than a hundred memos, what principles and level of performance you hold sacrosanct. I do not believe that leaders always have to be polite.

Nevertheless, a good leader takes each and every opportunity to train his people. One of the best ways to train them is to let them have the experience of taking charge when less than superlative performance can be tolerated. It is the way you encourage people to grow. At the same time, your people gain confidence in your leadership, for each time you correctly analyze a situation as not life-threatening and let them work the problem, your people gain renewed confidence in your judgment.

If everything is so critical it requires your personal intervention as a leader, you are destined to failure. First you will lose your followers. No one can maintain a pace of everything being of equal importance. Things simply are not. The care someone uses in combing his hair is not nearly as important as remembering to look both ways, every time, before he crosses a Manhattan street.

Let me give you an example from my profession. If you have never been in a submarine control room before this, let me explain that each of them is so laid out that there is one physical position from which, when he chooses, the commanding officer can stand and feel the entire fighting ship wrapped around him and at his fingertips as a glove is to a hand. When the commanding officer of the submarine steps into that spot behind the attack periscope and acts dictatorially, he instantly cuts through one or two levels of management. It is as if he bypasses the submarine's spinal nervous system and links his brain directly to each finger. A good commanding officer can stand in that one position and operate the ship with practically no other officer assistance. He can directly oversee the diving and control team, the sonar team, the navigation team, the fire control team, etc. And the good commanding officer knows that there are times when he must do this—when good men are beginning to panic from danger or sensory overload. When the situation demands that one precise move be made at one precise moment. When the ship is in danger and must be saved.

But just because it is possible does not mean it is desirable.

Every time the commanding officer takes control of his ship in this way he eliminates one training opportunity for his junior officers. Probably an excellent training opportunity—if the commanding officer but had the nerve. Another opportunity lost to let a young officer test his fledgling wings, an opportunity to walk close and peer over the edge—with the commanding officer's hand near his belt.

Leadership is often just standing back. Standing back and deliberately moving your branches aside so some sunlight gets down to the saplings. Giving your subordinates the time and the nourishment necessary for growth.

Let us return to our story. The commanding officer who would not let his officer of the deck even handle the underwater telephone had no patience and no interest in making people grow. He also was so protective of his own image, and wanted to appear so much in command, that he routinely acknowledged for messages not yet received and relied on Lady Luck to bring the missing information in on the afternoon wind.

Well, it worked two times out of three. He would have been great in the minor leagues.

As we continue the story, there is still another point of interest— for this was one of those events in life from which several lessons could be learned.

Let us review the situation. My submarine has, in violation of good sense and communications discipline, rogered for a message we had not received. Subsequently, as we didn't know where we were supposed to go to meet the other submarine, we didn't find her. At this point we compounded our error by (brazenly or foolishly) reporting that the other submarine was missing (and presumed lost).

The other submarine has followed proper procedures for using the underwater telephone, provided clear and direct guidance as was her responsibility as the senior submarine, and has been off doing her training, probably in a very professional manner.

Both ships were subsequently ordered to return immediately to port to discuss exactly what had happened. The commanding officer of our submarine performed a career-prolonging move—he developed his story into a brief, painted in living color. Along the way he perhaps used a little artistic license, shading some here, suffering a little loss of memory there, (especially about some "rogers" and "out").

He showed up at the informal inquiry armed with a colorful brief and an engaging smile. The other commanding officer showed up armed only with the truth.

I told you it wasn't a pretty story. I understand the other commanding officer was reprimanded.

Life is not necessarily fair. Sometimes what really happened is lost in the emotions of the moment and the inexactness of reconstruction.

However, don't waste too much of your sympathy on the reprimanded commanding officer. When he finally got his submarine back up to periscope depth and saw all of the high-precedence message traffic for him, he should have been quick to recognize that there was going to be some fallout. There were only two commanding officers out there in the ocean—it should have been easy for him to winnow down who were the candidates for the ceremonial hanging of the guilty. And there is no excuse if you let some son of a bitch beat you in the briefing room, especially when you have truth on your side.

Remember that some of the most worthless individuals can talk a good game. At the same time, some of the best people in the world are not natural speakers. So if you want to take the high moral ground, you have two choices. You can either let the bad guys walk away with victory whenever you bang up against them, or you can recognize that speaking skills are absolutely essential to those who aspire to leadership, and you can
> practice,
>> practice,
>>> practice.

There are several leadership concepts in this chapter that should have leaped out at you. If none has, let me gift-wrap one so you don't leave the chapter empty-handed. You should find this hint of particular usefulness: whenever you brief, do it in color.

# CHAPTER TWO

## Fear

Humans experience some very powerful emotions. None is stronger than fear.

People tend to wax long and loud about actions they have taken that they attribute to courage or love. Some individuals will even explain particular actions as the natural result of (justified) anger or their (socially desirable) instinct to be aggressive. However, we don't normally discuss actions taken as a consequence of fear. Strong executives don't like to admit they could be afraid.

In fact, I suspect that more than one of us would truly rather die than appear afraid. Which may not be all bad. Refusing even to recognize the possible existence of fear is sometimes a very useful organizational policy, especially in the military.

At the same time, every leader, including the military one, always needs to understand what is really occurring in the minds and hearts of his people. Frankly, fear is an integral part of many professions, including submarining. But, people are usually reluctant to acknowledge fear. Many consider fear no more interesting and no more suitable for open discussion than venereal disease. As a result, leaders often miss fear signals or misunderstand derivative emotional effects. Too bad. Recognizing the problem often dictates a solution.

When failures are difficult to explain, the experienced leader checks carefully for fear spoor around the water coolers.

Examples are plentiful. . . .

Once upon a time a submarine was undergoing overhaul. Like all submarine overhauls, this involved cutting holes in the pressure hull, removing important valves, pipes, and equipment, and disrupting nearly everything on board in order to make new modifications and check to ensure that the submarine components were still ready to support years more of continued operation.

Overhauls are tough on submarine crews.

First, the ship is ripped apart by people who don't seem to care about the effort the submarine crew has put into grooming their lady. Then the crew is forced to depend on the shipyard (which has the overwhelming bulk of the work force) to make key events on time. The submarine crew is used to being proud of getting each ship under way exactly on the minute advertised, no matter what the obstacle. The shipyard may not even intend to make the scheduled year.

Secondly, there is invariably someone or more in the shipyard who does shoddy work. Valves are installed backwards or not installed at all. Electrical insulation is not applied properly. Test results are dummied. The average citizen reads about examples of similar horrors in industry in his newspaper every week. In a submarine crew those actions would not be tolerated. The individual would be punished and then either retrained or drummed out of the submarine force. Makes sense. When a submarine goes down, everyone dies—not just the man who made the mistake.

Did you ever hear of a shipyard sinking? No? Well, then, it shouldn't be a surprise that when a mistake is made in an average shipyard the shipyard supervisors look the other way. Engineering supervisors are rarely leaders. They are more often managers. Thus, they usually decide that they can't actually decide exactly who is at fault, or, if the culprit is too obvious, they wrap themselves in the "union" jack. ("It's a problem, you see, with the union. They wouldn't allow us to punish him.")

Drives submariners nuts.

So, this particular submarine was being overhauled in a shipyard. And for reasons beyond the scope of this story, the overhaul, which should have been completed in about a year, dragged on for another couple.

Did I mention that the shipyard wasn't very close to any other Navy facility? Well, it wasn't. As the crow might fly, the shipyard was nearly a thousand miles from the nearest operating submarine base. There were several drawbacks to this geographic fact, but the most important one was related to the fact that travel funds are always limited in the Navy. Because the shipyard was so far away from the closest submarine base, it was expensive to get even the most routine training accomplished. Travel expenses alone were nearly five hundred dollars per man—if the man didn't eat or need a room.

Well, all things must end, even the most unpleasant. And after three years of working eighty to a hundred hours per week to accomplish very little tangible, you would think that this particular submarine crew would be very anxious to complete the overhaul and move to its next operating port, which was to be the pleasant little village of San Diego.

The last quarter or so of the overhaul effort is devoted to testing the things and systems that have been fixed or disturbed in the fixing effort. This is when you hope to find all the valves that have been installed backwards, or pipes that were not quite hooked up the right way.

Some overhaul repairs are just too difficult to test in port. For example, to test fully the weld on a patch covering a hole cut in the hull, there would have to be a tank big enough to put the submarine in (which would have to be about two football fields long and six or seven stories deep), and then a cover over the tank to permit all the water in the tank to be pressurized to simulate deep ocean depths. This is simply not feasible. Therefore, we X-ray the welds to look for cracks and foreign material, and if the pictures look good enough, we take the ship to sea and carefully and incrementally submerge it in Nature's own test vehicle—the ocean.

In this particular story, this submarine had completed all her testing alongside the pier and was getting ready to go to sea for sea trials. Once the submarine completed sea trials, it was going to be full speed ahead for San Diego.

There were eight divisions aboard this particular ship, and eight young officers assigned responsibilities for those divisions. Some of the officers were average. Some were below average. One was clearly superior. The superior officer knew the men in his division well. He knew their hopes as well as their failures. He knew his equipment and was nearly as qualified as his men to operate it. He treated his men firmly but fairly. He was uniformly excellent. In fact, you can list however many qualities you believe a good leader must have, and I will swear he had each one.

His people were above average. His leading petty officer was one of the finest I have known. Two of the nine other enlisted men later became officers, always a difficult and demanding path to success. The remaining seven were at least average.

But when it became time to get under way the only people who were there in this division were the officer, his chief, and the two people who would later become officers. The missing sent word from a local bar that they had some demands to be met before they would return to the ship.

Mutiny!

I thought about this incident for years.

We didn't give in on any of the demands. Giving in isn't the best way to run a railroad, much less a submarine. And, after we got back from sea trials without incident, the protestors had all lost heart in continuing their demonstration. They took their punishment quietly. Life went on. The event didn't even make the papers.

But why did it happen? What had we done so wrong that men would take a chance on the vagaries of the military justice system rather than do their duty? Why did it happen to our best division officer? Why did it happen on our ship?

It happened because we forgot about fear.

Aboard a submarine, nearly all the officers and crew are assigned to the ship for a tour of about three years. As there are about 140 people assigned, it means that each and every month you can count on bidding farewell to three friends and having about an equal number of new people report aboard. Each month, if all the new people turn out okay (and some of them inevitably fail to meet expectations), you acquire three new people who have never been to sea on your particular submarine. Three people who have never been stressed with your crew. Three people who may never have been as deep as a submarine normally operates. Three people who haven't been closed up in a pipe only nine yards in diameter and then propelled under the water for days and weeks.

We had been in overhaul nearly three years. We had fewer than a dozen old hands who had ever taken this ship to sea before. In fact, more than a third of the crew had never been to sea on any submarine before, much less a submarine they had personally watched being overhauled by a third-rate shipyard.

The men were scared. They expressed that fear with their feet.

It didn't matter that we had tested every run of pipe and box of electronics. It didn't matter that the officers and the crew witnessed every shipyard test and then often did the test again with only our own people involved. It didn't matter that we had crawled the ship hand over hand to ensure every bolt was put back together correctly.

You couldn't have ever made that crew comfortable. We tried. No luck. We had somehow managed to amass more than the critical amount of fear.

Consider this an Agatha Christie novel. You have all the clues. Who did it? Who or what created such an unsatisfactory situation?

The butler didn't do this one. This one was the complete responsibility of senior management on the submarine. Because we were so far from other operating ships, and because travel was so expensive, we had used all our funding in getting people to the required formal schooling. We had not thought about putting funds aside or making special arrangements to get people to ride other submarines. As a result, more than a third of the people on our submarine were going to go down to test depth for their first time—together.

They were going to watch the hull creep inward on them* while knowing that if anything went wrong a large portion of the crew was going to be of no help. Ugh! Even before we got under way the aura of fear was so thick it made all the compartments smell musty. In fact, so many people were afraid, they could almost talk to each other about their fear. Or at least they could all invent some bogeyman whom it was okay to fear: "That shipyard is so careless, I'll be gol-darned if I'm going to go down in that ship the first dive! Hey, another Bud over here."

That's what happened to us.

Well, some people are just born lucky. So, after a couple of years, on another submarine, I was involved with a very similar situation again. Our ship was in an extended overhaul ("extended" is shorthand for an overhaul that lasts years rather than months). The shipyard (a different one) was also at the nadir of its professional life, and we were again located in a corner of the country far from any other operating submarines.

---

* At deep depths, the submarine really is squeezed significantly by the pressure of the water. Some unkind, experienced soul always ties a string taut, head-high across the compartment. By the time the ship reaches test depth the compartment sides have been compressed inward so much the string is touching the floor. And the green people in the compartment have white faces.

Here was the ideal chance to see if we had learned anything from the last miserable experience. We had. We established one little rule. We insisted that each new person had to go to sea aboard another submarine within the first thirty days after he reported to us.

*Voilà!* Or "simple," as we midwesterners say.

Now nobody new had more than thirty nights to lie awake thinking how scared he would probably be the first time he went down in a submarine. Especially when he went down to test depth. No one had time to think how, even after a year on board, even after he was finally considered to be one of the boys, he would still probably puke and embarrass himself in front of his shipmates. Now each individual knew that he would make that particular professional hurdle without breaking. "Hell, I already went down there on *Usetafish,* and those sons of bitches weren't near as good as my buddies and me aboard *Myfish.*"

So the fear of fear went away. And the fear of going to sea in a submarine was ameliorated. Easy solution. Obvious. Once we identified the problem.

How did we pay for it? What about all those limitations I said we had on travel money? Good question, even if it is a bit nasty.

We simply decided the submerged at-sea experience was so important that everyone had to have it, no matter what the cost. Once that decision was made, over the next months several different people managed to think up affordable ways of making it happen. Another example of the adage (which we will discuss in another chapter) that any group can do one or two "anythings." You just have to want one or two particular anythings badly enough.

By the way, when our submarine finally completed this second overhaul, all of the supervisors commented about how the ship seemed so much more professional and competent than its sister submarines coming out of the same circumstances.

We also learned to work with fear in the day-to-day operating routine. Some people are afraid each time a submarine goes to sea. Thus, the smart submarine commanding officer tests his ship the first day under way, no matter how short or long the in-port period has been. He runs the engineering plant all the way up to its design limit. Then he puts the entire submarine through its paces at the maximum angles up and down. Finally he takes the submarine down to the deepest depth authorized—its test depth. Sometimes he varies the order, but the thoughtful commander never misses the routine. What has he really accomplished when he is through?

He has demonstrated to the entire crew, even those already trustingly asleep, that the ship will work as designed and that the man in charge is personally not reluctant to operate at those limits.

"He's not afraid. And goodness knows he can't put us at any more risk than he already has! Everything held together. Might as well get a bite to eat and grab some sleep."

What happens if the commander does not routinely operate his unit at design limits? Well, each member of the crew has a couple of options to think about in the privacy of his mind. "Either the unit can't—and if it can't, why doesn't someone fix it?—or the commander must know something I don't. Wonder what it is. Should we be afraid? Or worse, is he?"

Admiral Rickover understood this phenomenon very well. Many Americans don't realize it, but Admiral Rickover rode each and every nuclear submarine when it went out for its first dive. Why? Certainly not for the excitement. Initial sea trials aboard a submarine, as you carefully check the operation of every component, are very boring.

Not for the glory. Most of our submarines are built in New London, Connecticut. They often go on sea trials in the middle of winter. There is ice, snow, and wind in Connecticut in the winter. It is even too cold to take pictures. Rumor has it that national newspapers and TV stations don't even send reporters to Connecticut until spring.

Admiral Rickover went on each sea trial simply to demonstrate to everyone that he was not afraid. He believed his people had ensured each ship was built safely. But he knew that signing some certification paper was not enough. Admiral Rickover put his life on the line, every time, to show the crew he believed.

He went along to make sure you tested the ship to its design limits. Not just almost the design limits, but all the way up, and even past, so that you knew the submarine would always be there if you asked her to perform as the books said she would.

And what did Rickover do when something did not operate correctly on sea trials? Nothing. He would just walk to wherever on the ship appeared to be the most dangerous and sit down to watch the crew work. If the reduction gear sounded a little odd, he would go and sit on the reduction gear and ask the commanding officer to run the ship up to full power while the crew made a recording of the noise for analysis.

How could you be afraid when that little old man obviously was not?

Fear. Fear of losing your job. Fear of not getting a job. Fear of looking stupid. Fear of dying. Fear of being afraid. If you are reading this, you are in a profession that generates the emotions associated with fear. How do I know? Because, if there isn't danger, who needs a leader?

What does fear spoor look like in your job?

# CHAPTER THREE

# Winning

Success is often not correctly recognized as a leadership challenge. Success is traditionally considered a desirable result of good leadership, not a hurdle to be overcome. Yet success produces stress and tension that themselves often become the most difficult obstacles to continued success.

A good leader makes good decisions—time after time. The organization then comes to expect this as standard performance. The better the leader, the more the organization takes a continuous string of correct decisions for granted. They expect him always to be right. Their anticipation can grow so rapidly that the leader wonders if he can keep up the pace. That uncertainty (as to whether he can always be right) makes it much more difficult to keep making those good decisions. In fact, the stress can be such a heavy emotional and physical burden that even good leaders may actually turn aside from making decisions.

Such inaction can be destructive to the organization. A decision avoided is still a decision made.*

This chapter is about the pressure that builds as a result of doing anything well, including leadership. How do you recognize stress for the natural problem it is? How do you anticipate and prepare for it?

Unless you have been in a leadership position for some time you may not appreciate the problem. An example should ensure we are

---

* It might well be a *good* decision to wait. It is easy to visualize situations that are not yet ripe, or times when a leader might want to avoid closing out some options too early. But, nevertheless, a decision avoided is a decision made not to decide.

all thinking along the same lines. Perhaps an analogy from our national pastime?

In a baseball lineup every man has a role. The first man up is supposed to get on base—by a base on balls, being hit by the pitch, a bunt—however he can. The second man is tasked to advance that base runner. The third man in the lineup is usually the team's best hitter, someone who can be relied upon to get some action going on the base paths. Someone who can set the scene for the next hitter.

The next person in the lineup is the one we are interested in, for next we have the number four batter. The power man. The clean-up hitter.

What is his role? His role is to carry the day. The clean-up hitter is expected to produce when there are men on base. He is expected to break up ball games. A good clean-up hitter can lift his entire ball team nearly every day. And he is expected to do exactly that.

Not everyone has the emotional stamina to hit clean-up. Even in the major leagues very few teams have two men who can effectively hit as the number four man in a batting order.

Hitting fourth doesn't seem that hard to the average fan. If someone can hit, why should the order matter? Most clean-up hitters don't have an average as high as other hitters who precede or follow them in the order. Some don't lead their club in homers. No clean-up hitter ever leads in triples.

The average fan is often interested in helping his team's manager make out the lineup card. The fan calls into the talk shows: "Why does Manager Smith keep using only one guy in clean-up? There are two other players with higher averages. Hell, if you add Jones, there are three better hitters on the club!"

What there aren't, on any team, are two or three guys who can take the pressure of hitting fourth and still hit for average. There are few people who have both the tools and their own toolbox.

It is fascinating to see what happens if the manager of a losing team yields to fan pressure and substitutes someone else on the team in fourth place in the batting order. Almost inevitably the substitute starts to falter. His average steadily drops toward .200. His fielding suffers. The team continues to swoon.

Why? Simple. Expectations and stress. In baseball there is nearly a century of tradition that assigns the clean-up man the responsibility of being the team's big hitter. He carries that burden for everyone else on the team. His position in the batting order calls out loudly to each and every opposing pitcher, "show me your best stuff!"

If the clean-up hitter can hit the pitcher, that pitcher becomes easier for everyone else on the team to beat. I'm not sure why. It may be because the pitcher has put his best effort into pitching to the fourth batter and then relaxes. Perhaps the man on the mound loses his confidence. Maybe he actually tires after expending so much emotional and physical energy on the clean-up hitter. Whatever the cause, it happens, summer after summer and year after year.

There are very few men who can accept the stress of this responsibility for themselves and for their team. Most men, even major leaguers, will crumble if forced to hit fourth. At the same time, no team is competitive if it is missing a good fourth-place batter. Every good team needs a clean-up hitter.

So does every good organization.

The clean-up hitter in baseball is the closest analogy I can think of to the leader in an organization such as a military unit. The good organization leader never strikes out with runners in scoring position. The good leader never makes a bad decision about an important issue. The good leader routinely carries a streak that would make any DiMaggio envious.

But don't think establishing such a streak is easy. Being counted on to do well each and every time is a terrible strain. Most people cannot carry the burden.

Let's leave the sports category and I'll give you a professional example.

In the Navy the typical officer proceeds up the ranks from his initial grade of ensign, reaching the grade of captain (colonel in the Army or Air Force) after about twenty-one or twenty-two years of commissioned service. To get to that senior rank an officer has to pass successfully through six selection processes. Every three or four years a selection board (as it is called) meets to evaluate the comparative records of a particular officer and his contemporaries (his competition). Visualize the selection process as a pyramid. Near the bottom there are plenty of blocks to climb on to get ahead. Similarly, when an officer is very junior advancements come easily. On the other hand, as an officer gets closer to the top of the pyramid the opportunities for promotion get fewer. However, in my experience, if an officer works hard and keeps his nose clean and his reputation shiny, he has an excellent opportunity to be promoted to commander (that is, nearly everyone with the support of his or her peers makes commander), and will probably be promoted to captain (there are never enough billets available to promote every deserving commander to captain). So far, so good.

The rub comes with the next selection—to rear admiral or brigadier general. Suddenly it is as if the candidate had come to the base of a flagpole someone has placed on the apex of the pyramid. Using Navy figures as an example, while there is approximately a three in five chance of being selected for captain, there is only about a one in twenty chance of subsequently being promoted to rear admiral! Obviously many qualified and very deserving officers do not get promoted to rear admiral. While many exceptional captains are disappointed when they are not so selected, this process serves the nation well, for the country always has a ready supply of extra officers fully qualified to serve as admirals and generals. However, the process is not the point of this vignette. Instead, we are interested in the manner in which many captains behave as they approach that critical time in which they finally become eligible for selection to rear admiral (usually about twenty-five to thirty years after the day they walked out of college).

Each officer has worked very hard and well for nearly three decades. Each officer has moved self and family tens of times. Each officer has endured low pay and long hours in order to get to the top of his leadership position. Then, just as the selection is almost within his grasp—many captains simply remove themselves from the selection process!

A particular captain doesn't raise his or her hand, wave it for attention, and (honestly) say, "Hey, I don't believe I can stand the stress of competing where I am nearly bound to lose. I don't want to play unless there is an excellent chance of success. I don't believe I have enough self-confidence to fail (to make admiral). So just take my name out of the hat."

He doesn't do that. No one wants to admit to himself (or his peers) that he can't stand the stress of probably losing a competition.

Instead, the captain does something that will give him an excuse for the rest of his life. He either has an affair (the Navy is very conservative about morals, so that will make him unpromotable), or suddenly decides that he can't move to a different town (frequent moves are essential to the upwardly mobile officer). Or he may turn down an assignment (another no-no), even if it doesn't require moving, and, in fact, may be a very desirable assignment.

I know it sounds improbable, but I have seen more than one contender do each of these. I once watched a good friend, whom I considered an absolute cinch for promotion, turn down two excellent assignments, both in highly desirable locations, and then accept a lesser job in a location neither he nor his wife wanted. He would have been eligible for rear admiral the next year. Why did he do it? He knew his actions were professional death.

Why? Because, just like the hitters who can't bat clean-up, he couldn't stand competing when he wasn't likely to win. He couldn't accept the stress of probably and publicly failing.

The person who would be an exceptional leader has to become comfortable with being the person everyone always relies upon. The pressure isn't just for a week. The pressure is not just for a month. The stress for a real leader lasts day in and night out for decades.

The good leader routinely establishes a record difficult to appreciate fully. Think about it in baseball terms. In every baseball season several hitting or winning streaks develop. As each starts and gathers momentum, it accumulates press and fan interest like an autumn wind snatching leaves. However, usually within a week or two, no matter how good the player or the team, the streak collapses. Exceptions make covers for *Time* magazine.

Unlike their baseball peers, men and women who would be contenders for an organization's top jobs have to keep a streak going for years. How do they do it?

It is more than starting early and staying late. It is learning how to be comfortable with winning. Learning how to deal with the pressure of grand expectations, with the strain of stress.

I know of only one way to learn how to deal with stress. There is only one way to recognize what is happening when your throat gets tight . . . when your head seems faint . . . when your stomach curls itself tighter than a September pennant chase. You have to experience it. It isn't the flu. It isn't scarlet fever or Lyme disease. It is simply fear of being wrong.

To grow into a leader the individual has to learn that he will actually live through the effects of fear. Roosevelt was right. More is lost from fear of failure than from failure itself.

How does a person learn that he will actually survive the fear that seems so intense it will stop his heart from beating? Just as one learns most other things—practice.

Life is hard. People will always experience stress—win or lose. But if an individual can learn to accept the physical effects of stress, tighten his belt and his jaw, and continue on, the difference between success and failure is often only about another two inches of effort.

The person who is interested in leadership becomes involved in competition early. He or she learns what it is to lose. He learns what it is like to get beyond the limits that seem almost physically impossible to overcome. He learns what it is to win.

And when you have learned to win, then take the next step. Learn how hard it is to win as the favorite.

You will find it was almost sinfully easy to win as the underdog. It is not so soft as the favorite. Just as the best horse carries a heavier weight, the favorite carries the stress of expectation. As the front-runner you don't receive any praise for winning, or for a merely good decision. But you certainly get more than your share of criticism for losing. Sometimes you will be criticized just because the match was close. If you are the leader you certainly will be criticized later for any decision that turns out not to be the best that was feasible.

As the favorite you learn that being at the top carries with it the terrible burden of always performing—for the leader, this equates to always being right.

How do you learn to cope with the pressures of being the favorite, the stress of being the leader? By winning.

You can learn to win by playing chess, poker, checkers, by raising dairy cows for the county fair, by competing in beauty and talent pageants, through debate competitions, or anything else. You can learn to win in team sports, if your performance (or lack thereof) makes a real difference to the team. But, however you choose to compete, you have to try to win. You cannot settle for second or third, or just plan to participate. You must try for the grand prize and experience the stress of winning.

And the pain of losing.

Then decide which is more painful to you.

Remember well the anguish and pain of losing. Tie it up with a bow and store it somewhere in your heart. Blaze the path to the spot. Whenever you start to forget, you want to be able to peek in the box. The memory will help you fight through the stress of making decisions.

Good leaders are men and women who have practiced deciding. They are men and women who have faced the stress of making decisions many times. They recognize the physical and mental ghosts that rise like vapors from the cauldron labeled "the fear of being wrong." Leaders are men and women who can address these goblins by their first names.

Good leaders are those who stride around and past those who fear being wrong more than they enjoy winning. Leaders are those who can accept the stress of making the decisions as the public favorite.

Learn to win. Then, practice winning.

And while you are putting your own house in winning order, think about your subordinates. How do you teach them what you have learned about winning? In many organizations I served in, we had a problem keeping our good young officers in the service. Even when they had good supervision they left!

"I mean, their boss works at least twelve hours a day, six or seven days a week. And he is really smart. And knows nearly everything. In fact, there is quite a team on that ship. The executive officer is also a terrific worker. He works at least as hard as anyone aboard. Maybe harder! And the commanding officer is really good. He never makes a mistake. He is always on the ship."

Is that ship setting up a competition that the junior officer doesn't believe he can win? Is the junior officer leaving the organization to avoid possibly failing at the next higher level?

By working extremely long hours and just getting by (it is human nature to let everyone know how hard one is working and how difficult the job is), are the senior officers aboard that ship not subvocally telling the young officer that he cannot possibly do their jobs?

These senior officers aren't training and encouraging a young officer to advance. They are instead making that young worker believe it is probably impossible for him to move up. Look what it takes to succeed here! And the young officer doesn't want to fail. So he avoids the challenge. He leaves. Surprise?

It is not enough for the good leader to learn to win himself. The exceptional leader recognizes how stressful is life's "natural" competition. He thus makes efforts to eliminate or reduce unnecessary tension in the work environment.

Learning to win is important. But it is hard. The leader recognizes that difficulty. The good leader teaches important lessons by simply making winning possible for his subordinates.

# CHAPTER FOUR

## Nope

When things go well and awards are handed out, it is often difficult to determine just where to stop. Drawing the line for official recognition is a rather arbitrary process. This is especially true in team competitions. Many people can truly claim part of any success. When award time arrives, the surge toward the podium rivals a lemming migration.

The nomination field tends to trim itself when things do not go so well. By the time senior management realizes everything is not as it should be, investigates to determine exactly what happened, and decides to dispense justice, the dirt-packed arena floor is often clear of everything except empty chairs. Even those whose jobs placed them at the accident scene are usually now clustered over by the exits having a smoke.

As each party steps into the witness box to testify as to what he actually did or did not do, the neutral observer may see a little three-step foxtrot performed. The first step is the denial that the party actually should have recognized and avoided the danger (he wasn't there, it wasn't his department, it wasn't etcetera). If that doesn't serve to wiggle him quickly clear of responsibility, his second step is to blame his superior. If that also doesn't seem to work, the accused then usually points out that he cautioned his boss to avoid whatever it was that really caused the problem.

The last defense step raises an interesting question. Does this supposed warning absolve the individual from responsibility for the failure? Most participants appear to believe it should. They are often disappointed, if not downright shocked, if the appropriate tribunal doesn't promptly excuse them from responsibility for what followed.

For goodness sakes, why not? Just what exactly does a junior have to do when it is clear the ship is headed for the rocks but his boss absolutely refuses to listen to reason?

Good question. Is it possible for the junior to lead the senior? Is the junior responsible to do so? And where does the junior's responsibility stop? Perhaps a story or two, maybe three. . . .

In order to keep strategic submarines at sea (and thus invulnerable) a greater percentage of each year, from the very beginning of the Polaris program each strategic missile submarine has been manned by two separate crews. Each crew spends roughly half of the year on the ship, either alongside the pier working eighteen- to twenty-hour days conducting maintenance, or at sea working eighteen- to twenty-hour days operating the ship. The other half of the year the members of each crew are home with their families.

This story involves one of the crews on one of our strategic submarines.

We had to perform a particular maintenance evolution on the submarine. It was scheduled to be done while we had the ship, and therefore our crew could not be relieved until the evolution was completed (a little management device applied to make sure the hard jobs are not all passed on from crew to crew). Now, I am going to be a little vague about the particulars of this evolution because they turn out not to matter. If we could only have recognized the forest, it wouldn't have been necessary to tag each tree for identification during the later investigation.

Anyway, there were two options for performing this evolution.

Option one, which was the recommended one, required the ship to come into port in order to have scuba divers go over the side and hook up some auxiliary equipment to the ship below the waterline. After the auxiliary equipment was tested (which required about a day), the submarine would get back underway and return to sea to perform the evolution. The evolution itself required only a couple of hours.

Option two was a procedure that permitted the ship to do the hookup of the auxiliary equipment at sea.

The advantages to option two were obvious. If you hooked up the equipment at sea, you didn't have to drive the submarine all the way into port and then retrace your track back out (saving at least a day or two of steaming time). And because you did not have the necessary test equipment at sea, the normal testing (which we had heard was difficult to accomplish) was waived if you performed the evolution at sea.

Of course, you had to send divers over the side of the submarine out in the big, wide ocean, and due to some other preconditions the submarine had very limited mobility for the couple of hours the divers were over the side, but (and this was the driving reason for us) if you did the evolution at sea, you saved at least two days!

Instead of taking six days to turn over the ship after the patrol (two days for the evolution plus the normal four days for the other crew to nose around in our knickers and look for trouble), we could do the turnover in the normal four days and get back home two days early!

So we all talked about it. One of the officers was told to check and double-check the auxiliary equipment we would need. Finally, the ship's senior officers made plans that if the weather permitted, and if we could find somewhere in the sea where we could lie quietly on the surface and not be run over for a couple of hours, then and only then we would do this sucker at sea!

We went off on our seventy-day strategic deterrent patrol. Each week we reviewed our plans to conduct the evolution at sea so we would be ready if the chance came. Everybody on board became involved in helping to make sure everything would go well so we could save two days and get home early. The whole concept was terrific for morale. Everybody was working for a common purpose: to do something more efficiently and get home two days early.

We finished the patrol with our customary panache, and started back, looking for good weather and a quiet place. Along the way we practiced the ship operations that we would need to do to support performing the evolution at sea. We wanted to be ready if the chance came. And then luck was with us: perfect weather and no ships on the horizon!

We got everyone organized, shut down the reactor so we wouldn't inadvertently irradiate one of the divers, and got started. The first diver quickly splashed over the side.

And we were just as quickly in trouble.

At the time, we did not have equipment that would control the atmosphere inside the submarine to be exactly like the air out in the country. Or even like the air around Los Angeles. We could control the oxygen so it was the same as you are accustomed to breathing. We could usually even keep the carbon monoxide close. Our major problem was carbon dioxide. We were not even in the same ballpark with respect to keeping this breathing byproduct at normal levels. In fact, we had trouble getting carbon dioxide much below about sixty or seventy times the usual atmospheric concentrations. Over the years it didn't seem to hurt anybody too much. Some sensitive souls seemed to get a few more headaches. Everybody's blood clotted more slowly— a pinprick would take two minutes or more to clot. A serious cut required immediate attention.

Years later we found that an environment high in carbon dioxide also significantly affected human endurance. There are always unknowns. In many professions there is unrecognized danger ever present on either side of the marked and beaten path.

The fact that there was something we didn't understand was obvious within a minute after the first scuba diver went into the water. Before thirty seconds had passed he was exhausted. He was probably the strongest man aboard. A little obnoxious, perhaps a bit of a bully. Certainly proud of his strength.

Unfortunately he was also lazy and hadn't worked out during the entire time we had been on patrol. A submarine doesn't have any extra room allotted for working out. There isn't space. You have to make an extraordinary effort just to get any exercise. Most men don't bother. The ship's designated scuba divers are supposed to make a special effort in the event something unexpected happens. The first diver in the water had not done so.

As a result, he had immediately lost the mouthpiece on his scuba gear and was now flailing at the water in panic, and the weight of his oxygen tanks was dragging him under.

Concurrently we were now finding just how hard it was on a submarine to pull someone back up out of the water. We hadn't drilled on actually putting someone in the water. A submarine is round all the way around the hull. It is also round up on the top. In fact, there is damn near nothing up there to get any purchase on. All wet, with his equipment, the diver weighed nearly five hundred pounds. There were four people topside trying to balance on top of the submarine and simultaneously pull up five hundred pounds of struggling, panicky man.

I was watching through the periscope.

The senior enlisted man on board a submarine is always especially selected for his job. He is expected to lead the enlisted crew by example, by force of personality, and also to perform many officer tasks.

His unique position in the submarine force is denoted by a unique title, for while there may be several senior enlisted individuals aboard a submarine (or "boat," in the vernacular) who have reached the top three rates of chief petty officer, there is only one who is referred to as the chief of the boat, or COB in Navy lingo, pronounced as in corn.

Our chief of the boat was truly an exceptional man. He was very experienced, had previously been a qualified diver, and even in the small confines of a submarine, always kept his body tuned. At this moment, he was assisting the officer who was directing the effort from the submarine's deck. When the COB saw the deck team having difficulty in pulling the diver up out of the water, he dove in the ocean and began pushing the struggling diver upward, using his strong legs in a scissors kick to produce a powerful upward thrust.

This helped significantly. On the next wave the diver was pulled up two feet—almost all the way up on deck. As the support from the wave retreated, he slipped back a few inches. Everyone pushing and pulling took a deep breath and waited for the next wave to help carry the diver up to safety atop the deck. Meanwhile, through the magnification of the periscope, I could see the diver's face as if I were within a foot. He had lost all composure. He was simply terrified of falling back in the water. On the next wave he suddenly slipped the heavy oxygen tanks from his shoulders, and with the dramatically reduced weight was quickly pulled up and safely aboard.

The two hundred pounds of steel and oxygen fell back and crushed the skull of the senior enlisted man in the water below. As I watched in horror, the COB's swimming motion ceased. He slid back flat in the water, his face expressionless, his eyes open. Lifeless, he slowly began to sink below the waves.

Suddenly we noticed a ship on the horizon. It was headed directly towards us. We had been distracted by the drama on deck. It was a large tanker. A submarine, even a strategic submarine, makes a very small target on the surface. The tanker would never see us. We needed to get underway and move. Too bad we had shut down the reactor.

Another crew member who had also kept himself in shape dived in the sea and, disregarding the shark fin that appeared as soon as the skull was crushed, swam down about twenty feet and retrieved the COB's body. We wrapped the body in black plastic and put it in the submarine's walk-in refrigerator. We would have to keep it there until we returned to port.

There were no problems starting up the engine room, and we moved safely off the tanker's track. The ship never did notice us. As often happens in the open ocean aboard large commercial ships, there did not appear to be anyone on the bridge.

When we got into port and installed the auxiliary equipment alongside the pier, we found that the officer who had supposedly checked to ensure we had all the parts had done a poor job. The components that locked the apparatus together were missing. Remember that the at-sea hookup procedure didn't test the setup. We had been lucky. If we had tried to use it, the rig would have fallen apart with disastrous results.

We had been lucky. We had killed only one man.

And even though I had not had direct responsibility for deciding to do this evolution at sea, or for checking the test rig, or for making sure the divers stayed in shape, or for picking the spot to perform the evolution, I was the one who got to watch the senior enlisted man die. I was the one who lay in my bunk at night and remembered how his black eyes had suddenly gone dull.

And thought about how I should have said that I didn't care if we got home two days later. I mean, we all knew there was some danger in doing the thing at sea. If we had done it the conservative way, it would have meant only that we would be away from home one more percent that year. If I didn't think the risk was worth it, why didn't I let everyone on board know I disagreed with them? People like consensus. Most people, even in an organization supposedly as autocratic as the military, won't act without it. Why didn't I destroy consensus? Why didn't I make everyone a little uncomfortable about acting? It probably would have been enough to keep us from doing the evolution at sea.

I knew that the officer assigned to check the test rig was ineffective. Why hadn't I checked behind him? I knew the first diver in the water was lazy. Why hadn't I mentioned that the diver hadn't been exercising?

Well, it wasn't my place. First, none of what we were doing fell into any area of my responsibility. Second, I was the junior officer on board. So, who would expect for me to speak out? I mean, they would think I was a fool. There. That should help me sleep.

Second story.

Once upon a time, a submarine was out in the wide, wide ocean providing services for antisubmarine airplanes. For these particular services the submarine would run a predetermined course for two hours while the airplane practiced tracking it, and then the submarine would come back up to periscope depth, establish communications, discuss how the last two hours of training had gone, and get instructions on what should be done for the next two hours.

We do this sort of exercise all the time. Did then. Still do. Nearly exactly the same way. We provide the airplane a real submarine target, in real seawater, and we can even get in some training for ourselves at the same time. With a little prior thought, the submarine can conduct routines that require it to be shallow and at slow speed during the period the airplane is passing instructions for the next event. Drills and evolutions that don't affect propulsion can then be performed while you are down deep following the track the airplane has specified. Routine operations. Purely routine. For both the airplane and the submarine.

Now, you also need to know that a nuclear submarine has one or two diesel engines to use for emergency power. The diesels are not terribly powerful, and certainly don't provide all of the power you normally need, but they do provide enough power to enable you to shut down the reactor when you are in port, even in ports without electricity. Other times the diesels are useful when you want to do something to the engineering plant that requires the reactor to be turned off at sea.

The diesels on this particular submarine were a difficult design. They had not originally even been intended for use aboard a submarine. As one result they were terribly tough to keep tuned. Every couple of days, when we got a minute while we were surfaced or at periscope depth, we started them up and adjusted their timing so they would work when we needed them. Routine evolution. Routine practice.

The first time we tried to start them that day, we applied fuel and high-pressure starting air, and nothing happened. A common problem with a diesel with a bad timing sequence. The pressure generated in the cylinders was high, but not quite high enough to generate an explosion. We got some combustion, but not quite as much as we needed to get a twelve-foot-long diesel engine rotating smoothly at several hundred revolutions per minute.

We didn't have any better luck the second time we tried.

Nor the third.

The airplane called up and said that he was now ready, and we were to go down to several hundred feet and head east on the track he had specified. The commanding officer turned to the officer of the deck and said to hurry up and comply.

Now we had a problem.

When a diesel engine fires it needs lots and lots of air. It essentially takes the air from the submarine atmosphere, combusts the fuel using that air, and pushes the exhaust gases out under the water. Fresh air from outside the ship comes in the submarine via a large mast (called the snorkel mast) to replenish the air inside the submarine.

When the diesel doesn't quite fire, it doesn't generate enough pressure to force any of the exhaust gasses out of the submarine. Unfortunately, when the diesel almost but doesn't quite fire, it also generates lots of carbon monoxide, a colorless, odorless, highly toxic gas. A bad gas to have aboard submarines. Carbon monoxide—without any preliminary indications—quickly causes people to pass out. Aboard a submarine you can't quickly run out of the garage to get fresh air. Particularly if that submarine is several hundred feet below the surface.

The diesel engine aboard this submarine had been generating carbon monoxide at a rate equivalent to running about a hundred cars inside one garage. It had done so only for a few seconds each time. But we had tried to fire the diesel three times. There was no way to tell quickly if there was a problem. The safe thing to do would be to ventilate the ship—to pull a lot of clean air in the ship and purge the old air out. It would take about thirty to forty minutes. By that time we would also be able to have someone conduct the chemical test for carbon monoxide to verify whether we had a problem.

The commanding officer was a very impatient person. He wanted to appear absolutely professional. He wanted to appear dynamic. He wanted to appear dynamic even to the junior lieutenant above us flying his airplane. The commanding officer especially wanted to appear dynamic to whoever might read any message this lieutenant might send about training delays the submarine had caused. The commanding officer told the officer of the deck to submerge immediately. We would ventilate the ship to get rid of any noxious gases after we had run the next two-hour track.

Possibly that approach would be safe.

It would be okay if the diesel had not actually generated very much carbon monoxide.

Of course, if the diesel had generated too much carbon monoxide, someone might die. We all might.

Going deep before ventilating would never be termed very prudent.

The officer of the deck thought the problem over. He then called the commanding officer on the telephone and quietly explained the options and risks as he saw them, and recommended that the ship be ventilated before going below periscope depth.

The commanding officer told him to "go deep" as he had previously been ordered. And "be quick about it."

The officer of the deck called the executive officer, explained the situation, and asked the more senior officer to intercede.

Within a few seconds the commanding officer called the officer of the deck back and very explicitly told him that he did not appreciate his judgment being questioned, and wanted "this ship taken deep—now! Without further discussion!"

We need to take another slight sidetrack. There are lots of official records aboard a submarine. As a submarine is a stealth vehicle and provides our national deterrence against our major enemies, we don't like people to know anything about where submarines have been or what we have done. Thus, nearly all the records aboard are classified at least confidential. There is one record that is deliberately not classified—the deck log.

The deck log lists which officer is responsible for the ship at which times, and when that responsibility shifts, and some other specific things such as whenever someone is injured. Thus the deck log provides, open to anyone and everyone, an unclassified record trail for legal matters. The deck log answers questions that don't involve classified answers, such as:

"Who was officer of the deck at the time the grounding occurred?"

Look in the deck log.

"Was my son, Seaman Grunk, ever hurt while working on a torpedo? He wants to apply for disability benefits."

Look in the deck log.

And the officer of the deck in this little story, thinking it over again, and believing the issue could well be one of life and death, decided to lay his career on the line. So he picked up the deck log and he wrote:

I have reason to believe that we may have a high carbon monoxide concentration in the ship, and have recommended to the commanding officer that we immediately ventilate the ship in order to prevent loss of life. Disregarding that advice, the commanding officer has ordered me to take the ship deep in order that we meet routine training requirements.

And the officer of the deck signed his name, along with the exact time and the date. And he ordered a messenger to take the log to the commanding officer and request that the commanding officer read and countersign the entry.

Less than a minute after the messenger left the room, the commanding officer called the officer of the deck, "Ventilate the ship, you son of a bitch, and when you find out what the carbon monoxide concentration actually is—call me." The messenger of the watch reported that the commanding officer had ripped the page from the deck log.

Fortunately for the officer of the deck, shortly after the submarine started ventilating two men collapsed from the effects of carbon monoxide poisoning. In the cleaner, ventilated air they soon recovered.

The appropriate page of the deck log was recopied. This time it omitted the officer of the deck's precipitous (and propitious) entry. Nobody died. Nobody was hurt. Only two or three people even knew of the disagreement. The commanding officer never mentioned the subject again. Within half an hour the ship had returned to routine operations.

Third story.

Once upon a time there was this submarine that had a wardroom of about sixteen officers. One officer was the commanding officer, who was, of course, in charge of everybody. Then there was the executive officer, who worked directly for the commanding officer and as usual, while theoretically in charge of everyone else, actually did all of the administrative work and those other jobs the commanding officer didn't care to do.

There were also three primary department heads aboard, all officers serving their second tour aboard submarines. Each of the department heads had responsibility for a large section of the submarine: engineering, operations, or weapons. The rest of the dozen officers in the wardroom were on their first submarine, had been aboard for different periods of time ranging up to four years, and were assigned to work for one of the three department heads.

The story revolves around the personality of the commanding officer.

He did not like to be wrong. He could not tolerate criticism. He could not abide failure. Or perceived indecision.

I once saw him fire someone who had a slight stutter and had learned to correct that stutter by hesitating slightly before he spoke. The commanding officer attributed that hesitation to indecision. The commanding officer never asked if there might be another reason. Nor did he apparently think about it. He just fired him. The officer he fired had more than ten years experience in submarines and had always been very successful. The commanding officer fired the officer one day when the latter hesitated momentarily before explaining why he had done an evolution a particular way.

The commanding officer fired a lot of officers out of that wardroom. At that time the submarine force didn't question the personnel actions of commanding officers very hard. We didn't hold commanding officers sufficiently responsible for personally training their officers. We didn't look askance if a commanding officer had to fire more than one or two officers in the commanding officer's three-year tour.

This particular commanding officer fired nearly a dozen officers in two years.

He had learned that whenever the wolves got near the sled the easiest solution (for him) was to cut the throat of the weakest dog and leave it behind on the trail. In this case, for wolves substitute the questions of superiors about the performance of the ship. For the weakest dog substitute the weakest officer in the wardroom.

Obviously there are a lot of unanswered questions here about people who can't stand the heat rising to leadership positions in careers in which there are always new situations and challenges, constant pressure, and absolutely no chance to be right and successful every time.

This commanding officer should have been a farmer where I was born. In Indiana, if you throw corn seed on the ground, cover it with manure, and let God rain on it when he wants, you inevitably get a useful crop. Not every job is like that. In the submarine force the very best officers are never successful more than about half the time. There is too much uncertainty. The ocean is a tough pitcher—Cy Young class. What you really ask for in jobs like those is a majority of small wins and no big losses.

This particular commanding officer was in the wrong business.

But what this story is really about is how the commanding officer was prevented from doing even more damage.

One of his department heads decided that the process was unfair, and that if the commanding officer's superiors were not going to do something about it, he, the department head, would.

His method was simple. When things went wrong (note that the operative word is *when*, not *if;* things always go wrong in any profession worth your time), the commanding officer typically began a lengthy informal selection process to determine which dog would be cut from the traces and thrown to the wolves. The commanding officer, like nearly everyone, liked to have consensus.

So the commanding officer would begin pointing out a particular officer's mistakes and instances of poor judgment. He would begin assigning the same officer all of the tasks that looked too hard to solve. He began publicly assessing all that officer's work as below standard. The commanding officer brought his presence to bear on the wardroom to cause the other officers to look away from the intended victim. To pick other people to sit next to. To laugh when the commanding officer encouraged laughter at the selected victim's expense.

Normally it took about three months to select the proper victim, destroy his confidence and esteem, and have him prepared for the next wolf threat. Three months to force consensus on the wardroom. All the officers could see it coming.

The department head decided to use his knowledge of that pattern to stop these miscarriages. When it became obvious that the commanding officer was looking for his next casualty, if the department head felt the intended victim was, or had the potential to be, a good and useful officer, he took that officer into his own department by saying, "Captain, I have noticed you have some concerns about Ensign Door. I think he can be saved. I would like to work with him. I will give up Lieutenant Window (the department head's best officer) to take charge of Door's division."

Then the department head shielded the junior officer. And mixed the junior's reports with other officers' and his own. And gave him tasks he could do successfully, for which he was praised. And kept from him the problems that couldn't be solved.

Now the commanding officer could not reach his selected victim without first taking out the department head. Of course there was always the real possibility that the department head would be out on the streets himself, looking for a new job, but there are always people who need pick-and-shovel work done, and it is much, much better to have to dig ditches between jobs than to spend your entire working life hiding in one, afraid to raise your head because you might draw fire.

And so life in this particular wardroom stabilized. Although the commanding officer's seniors were not effectively supervising him, the department head had managed to insert himself in that role. A junior officer had accepted responsibility for the performance of his senior.

Let me see if yet another story can bring this all together. Two hundred years ago in the West, there was an Indian tribe that practiced a pretty sophisticated sort of negotiation. When they believed in the overwhelming importance of an issue, such as the sanctity of a particular hunting area, they communicated that stand in a manner that could not be misunderstood.

When a war party from another tribe was reported on the way, the Indians first found a location that blocked access to the hunting area. A valley or meadow between two ridges was perfect. They wanted an area in which they could be seen clearly from far away, and that was devoid of cover. Then each man looked for a particular rock—one bigger than two fists, longer than it was wide. After selecting individual fighting positions stretching across the choke point, each dug a narrow hole at his position. The holes were dug straight down for about two feet, and were only wide enough for the rock to fit easily.

Then one end of a twenty-foot strip of rawhide was tied around the rock, which was lowered into the hole. Dirt was carefully tamped down on the rock and around the rawhide strip. The other end of the rawhide was then tied to the Indian's testicles.

An advancing enemy war party could not mistake this signal. These Indians would not break and run. There would be no easy victory. These Indians intended to die before giving up this hunting ground.

If the advancing war party did not care to compete in hand-to-hand combat to the death, it was up to them. They could choose not to engage.

Of course, there was a downside. If the Indians had misjudged the size of the opposing war party, or the size of the war party's hunger, the men making the stand could well all be overrun and killed.

How is this history lesson about early America related to leadership? This way. If you are convinced that you are right about an issue, if you believe that not following your recommendation will result in the violation of something terribly important, for which there can be no compensation or reparation,* then it is not enough just to say "Nope, I don't believe you should do that."

You have to be prepared to sacrifice your professional life and career.

---

* On the order of the death or emotional destruction of an individual, or (at least in submarines) the placing of the submarine in danger or the violation of a nuclear safety rule.

I do not encourage this practice. Compromise is most times the best, as well as the most acceptable, solution. If you don't like the direction a compromise is headed in, then acting to prevent the development of consensus is usually effective. If you do have to lay your professional life on the line more than once every couple of years, you may well be undervaluing your professional life. You are also probably overestimating the importance of the issue.

The great, great majority of the conflicts in life are solved in the normal ways humans and bureaucracies solve those things. But, on the other hand, every now and then, on a life-and-death issue, unless you lay your professional life on the line to prevent the mistake you are as responsible morally as the person who bumped against the initial domino.

When you do decide there is an issue on which you absolutely have to make a stand, be sure you don't waste your silver bullet. There are three basic rules. First, make sure no one can get to the objective down another path. Only a fool enters possibly deadly conflict when there is an alternative. Second, stand out in the open. Give your opponent a chance to choose not to join the conflict. Third, make sure your position is crystal clear. You don't want to force your boss to cough up a baseball only to then find out you would have been satisfied with a strawberry.

If you do wager your professional life and your bet is taken, you have done your job. You have cautioned your boss. If disaster then strikes, maybe you will be able to sleep at night.

On the other hand, if a casualty occurs and you have not laid your professional career on the line, look for a good lawyer. And pray for a dumb judge.

Don't ask for me.

# CHAPTER FIVE

## Growing

I am now old enough that young people just starting their careers often ask what they should do in their first job—especially if that job is aboard a submarine. They want to know how they can get their careers off to a good start. I can remember wondering the same thing.

*What a change! Never have held a really serious job. Goodness knows, four years in the hallowed halls of Lovely State don't count for much. I'm not even sure whether I should salute the flag first and then the officer of the deck or vice versa. They may not even let me aboard.*

*If I do get aboard, they are going to give me an impossible job. I'm to tell some guy older than my father what he is supposed to do. He was doing this job before I was born. What happens if he laughs? When I'm giving orders, how will I know men aren't smirking behind my back? Why in the world is the Navy organized this way—with officers right out of school in charge of people?*

Let's deal with the organization question first. We are organized this way because it works.

It is not efficient for all communications or leadership to be provided right from one senior executive directly to all the worker bees. It is much more effective for the senior to speak directly to a relatively small group of middle-level managers—his officers in this case—and then have each of these officers be responsible for relaying guidance and transposing the senior's desires into more specific action for his respective division. Big groups can't easily question unclear advice, or remind the senior about some circumstances or schedule he may have forgotten, or talk about the necessary coordination required between work centers.

In addition, young executives need to get a quick start on the most important part of their education—learning how to lead people. Anyone can master how to read a print or plan, repack a steam valve, or cut a set of slip rings. The difficult part of being a leader is learning how to get the best from your people. How do you sense and gauge their temperaments? When do they need to be stroked? When is the time to criticize? When should we quit work, even though the job is not done? When is it best to work through the night?

These decisions need judgment. Judgment improves with experience. Experience comes from what is commonly called "time in the chair."

And you need to seize every opportunity to get time in the chair. I know that it seems completely unbelievable to a recent college graduate, but you have a very limited time to gain the experience you will need to be prepared for senior positions. Most organizations, and especially the military, are a young man's game. If you are in submarines, by the time you are forty-five you are already too old for sea duty. You won't last in shore jobs much longer. Only admirals are permitted to stay longer than thirty years in the Navy. Twenty or thirty years seems longer than forever when you are young. When you are my age, you realize that it was a wholly inadequate slice of time. You had to hit the ground running to fit in all you are going to need.

The young executive who hopes to be competitive for selection to the very best (most challenging) jobs later in his career must get experience in different areas of the world, should get advanced schooling, needs duty ashore as well as at sea, and needs experience on staffs. He has very limited time to learn to work with people. The young officer can ill afford to lose one day of experience when the opportunity is available.

This need for experience is an excellent reason to place a young officer immediately in a leadership position with a division of sailors.

*Well, okay, maybe there is good reason for the assignment,* you might think, *but I still don't know how I am going to avoid making a fool of myself.*

To begin with, you are going to be surprised how busy everyone is—much too busy to waste time watching you. Although many of the people working for you are not terribly different in age or capability from your high school classmates, there is one important difference. They aren't all bored with school, standing in groups smoking and joking, shifting their weight from one foot to the other, waiting for a new green officer. They are instead working every minute. In any workplace worth working there is always more work than pairs of hands available to do it.

Your arrival will thus be largely unnoticed. People are curious about a new officer, but they are most interested in what the officer can and will do to make their lives easier. No one expects you to be the pre-eminent technical expert immediately. However, your people and your supervisors do expect you to start caring about your people immediately. They expect you to take responsibility for being a good traffic cop on leadership's two-way street. Your seniors expect you to explain to your people what the command demands and to reflect your people's concerns back up to the appropriate level reliably.

Representing your people doesn't require a lot of special experience. It does require a great deal of effort. It does require that you accept moral responsibility for doing enough and doing what is right for your people. You have to do it all for them. You have to keep track of when they need to apply for special programs, fight for appropriate special recognition for them, and accept the unpleasant task of telling them when their efforts are not adequate.

Whatever your job, whether it is your first or tenth assignment, you start by looking out for your people first. People are always your initial priority. It is a good lesson to get right in your first job.

If you start correctly by becoming involved with your people, the rest of your job is easy. I can even give you one single rule to observe—the "less comfort" rule. You can faithfully follow that rule by always listening carefully to your mind. Your mind, just like everyone else's, is a very capable calculator. Long before you even consciously begin to evaluate a problem, your mind has already computed the relative comfort of different possible courses of action. If you are sitting in your stateroom working on an overdue report and someone calls to tell you that they have found the problem with the steam leak— a galled shaft—your mind completes its analysis before you even hang the phone back on its hook.

What do you think your mind has come up with? Is it more comfortable to continue to sit in your stateroom with your cup of coffee and complete your overdue report so the executive officer won't bitch any more and you can get some sleep? Or is it more comfortable to get up from your chair, walk back, and look at the valve?

There is only one way you are going to find out what a galled shaft really looks like and how it affects the packing and packing follower. There is only one way you are going to be able to compliment (when it counts and when it is most effective) the tired machinist who disassembled the valve and found the problem that others overlooked.

And while you are back there holding the shaft in your hand, someone calls out from the bilge that they have found the trouble in the bearing race. The supervisor looks up from the dirty paperwork he is laboring over and tells the unseen voice to try to peen it over.

You have three choices. They are, in order of comfort: ignore the voice, ask the supervisor to put away the paper and explain the repair process to you, or get down on your back, scrunch under the pump down into the dirty bilge, bang your head twice on a valve, burn your arm just above the elbow on a steam pipe, and see exactly what the man is doing with that hammer.

If you ignore the voice, you are never going to make it as a supervisor. You may be a nice person. You may look nice in khaki. But you are certainly no leader. Find a job in a field that uses your other assets.

If you ask the supervisor to explain what he meant, you may make it as an officer.

If you get down in the bilge, you will probably ruin your uniform.

The bilge is the only place that will significantly broaden your base of knowledge. It is the only place to learn to lead. In the bilge you will better understand the high rate of failure common to this particular type of repair. You will understand how difficult some repairs can be. You will have a better feel for how equipment should be designed and arranged.

The bilge of a submarine is always an uncomfortable place to be. It is often dirty and always cramped. In this context, it stands for wherever in your organization is physically unpleasant. If you enjoy and are comfortable standing in any particular place, that location probably should be caution-posted as a low-learning area.

Why is this personal experience so important? Because in your first job you are soaking up experience that must last you for the rest of your life. Young managers have a limited amount of time in which to gather experience. During your first few years you aren't selective. You take in all sorts of raw data. Which is good. However, that pace soon slows. You become more selective as to information which you will accept. You begin making decisions as to how you will classify and index information in your mind.

These indexing decisions are essential to helping you apply old experience to new situations. They are part and parcel of the learning process as we understand it. However, there is a distinct downside. The minute you start indexing and evaluating your information, your perspective is both changed and limited. You are no longer accepting the same amount of new information as you did when you believed everything under the sun was important and relative.

The young executive consciously trying to experience as many professional challenges as possible is involved in the process of storing up samples he can later evaluate using the lifetime of experience he will accumulate. Twenty years after that night when you lay in the bilge and for the first time contemplated the relationship of available space and quality of maintenance, you will be relying on that experience in making decisions about the spacing of machinery in the design of a new submarine.*

Your trip to look at the galled valve stem has served another purpose. People have seen you are truly interested in their work.

People you work with are always going to talk behind your back. You can't stop it. They won't stop it. People are interested in people. They talk about other people. That night they will talk about you. They will talk about how much you care.

Always select as your option the low item on your mind's comfort index. Your mind won't let you down. It's reliably lazy. Remember, being a good junior officer is simply a matter of getting up from your chair or bed, walking to the scene, and then getting down and dirty.

Learning to run a division is mind over sleep.

---

* Admiral Rickover understood this principle exceptionally well. When the *Nautilus*'s reactor compartment was being built, he personally positioned himself at each valve and piece of machinery to ensure there was enough room to perform the maintenance which might be required. Excellent idea! However, some years later I often swore at him for not realizing that there were a limited number of men in the average crew who were five-foot-four and ninety-seven pounds or whatever the hell he was.

# CHAPTER SIX

# Patterns

We all find it downright interesting the way the human mind works. While standing in the grocery line, there is nothing we will more quickly read than some little article that hints at explaining something about our mind, such as why we can't remember a name that is "right on the tip of our tongue."

This is a healthy intellectual interest. Just as the aspiring auto mechanic is interested in the relationship between piston and crankshaft, the leader is interested in how humans think. If we understand the manner in which the mind takes in, stores, and recalls data, we should be able to teach more effectively. If we appreciate the limitations and power of the thinking process, we should also improve our own performance.

It can't hurt to understand better why we easily compose solutions to some sets of problems and yet labor long and hard with others that seem much more simple.

Let's plunge in. I have a hypothesis. If I am correct, this is a potential leadership gold mine.

Humans, that is, you and I, appear to do most of our thinking through a process of pattern recognition. We see a situation and it reminds us of something we saw before, or learned about, or read about. Maybe the relationship isn't exact, but it is close enough for a mind to see a parallel. We see an animal with four legs and a long body and extrapolate that it probably has a long tail. We see a roughened piece of metal in a machine and postulate that the area must not be getting enough lubricating oil. We see someone stagger on the street at night, and look immediately for a paper bag in his hand.

Exceptionally perceptive individuals may even observe the world in general and decide that human flight should be possible, postulate the concept of gravity, or that a relationship between energy forms exists. On the other hand, most of us observe life like a color-blind person looking at pages of blue-green and chartreuse dots. We don't see a pattern, even if someone hints or plain out tells us there is a picture or number hidden therein.

We recognize that people have different conceptual capabilities. A very few, such as Michelangelo, Newton, Darwin, and Einstein, quickly perceive patterns and relationships. For the rest of us, as was true of the frogs Darwin found on the Galapagos Islands, some are a tad bit slower than others.

Why are patterns important to a leader? To begin with, if an individual believed in pattern recognition it would influence how he taught. For example, a football coach would run football plays over and over to teach both offense and defense to recognize and react to patterns. A person concerned about developing a democratic public would recommend the study of history as a building block for thoughtful citizens.

Yes, you say, we already do all this.

Well then, are there other predictable pattern recognition problems leadership can affect?

Interesting question. Look at it from a negative viewpoint. If thinking is largely a process of pattern recognition, there are a couple of obvious ways to impede that process.

One way to disrupt thinking would be to create a background so abnormal, such as unusual surroundings, like the footprints of a polar bear in the Amazon, that the mind has difficulty accepting the pattern as reasonable, even if the prints are easily observed and well defined. A second way to disrupt thinking would be to obscure the prominent features of an object. Without key characteristics to recognize, the mind would see no pattern.

The good leader should obviously do whatever is possible to minimize development of these two disruptive situations.

Perhaps an example or two would be useful.

Once upon a time we submariners were worried about how a submarine would recover in the event one of her pipes ruptured, thus permitting seawater to flood into the ship. This was not an idle fear. In peacetime, up through the fifties, we had lost a submarine (and her crew) about every five years, usually from a casualty (a disaster) that started or ended with flooding.

Flooding is a submarine's worst threat. The potential for flooding is always present. At the same time, flooding destroys the submarine's only unique military advantage. A submarine cannot remain submerged and stealthy if it is flooding. It must surface to survive. Yet without the advantage of stealth the submarine is very susceptible to attack. In the worst circumstances, a submarine forced to retreat to the surface would be only seconds away from sure destruction.

Living under water keeps submariners always conscious of the danger of flooding. Not being complete dummies, we have spent a lot of time planning how to minimize the danger. It turns out that speed is important for survival. We can generate large lifting forces by putting an up angle on the ship and using that big nuclear reactor to drive the submarine right up out of the water.

But what if we lose speed for some reason?

Then the only safety margin left will be the rate at which we can push water out of the ship. If we can get the submarine up on the surface before more water floods in than we push out, we are going to live to fight another day. If not, we're not.

To get water out of the ship a submarine uses air pressure to blow water out of the ballast tanks.* High-pressure air is introduced into the ballast tanks at the top, where the air displaces the water, pushing it out the open holes on the bottom of the tanks. It is a simple system, but it doesn't solve the flooding problem very well.

Physics drives the situation. Because we are using air at high pressure to blow water out, the deeper the submarine is initially, the lower the differential pressure is between water in the sea and the stored high-pressure air; thus, the slower the rate at which water can be blown out of the ballast tanks.

Working against the submariner at the same time is the fact that the deeper the submarine operates, the faster the water floods in (for

---

* The submarine also has a pump that is normally used to pump bilge and other wastewater overboard. In addition to using high-pressure air to blow the ballast tanks, in a major flooding casualty the ship would also pump, but the pump capacity is so relatively small that pumping has only a secondary effect.

the same size hole, the flooding rate at two hundred feet is four times the flooding rate at one hundred feet—at four hundred feet the flooding rate is sixteen times higher). As a result, every foot the submarine goes deeper makes a flooding casualty that much more dangerous.

On the other hand, the submarine often operates better tactically if it is deeper.

All of us in the submarine force considered these facts and worried about them for years. Then someone had a bright idea—if, when we were to go deep, we operated with the submarine ballasted light (water deliberately pumped out from an in-trim condition), then if we lost power the submarine would go in the safe direction—up!

At the same time, if water started flooding in when we were trimmed light, it would take longer for the submarine to become heavy enough to sink. Time is of the essence when the ship is flooding. Every minute extra is sixty more seconds to try to stop the flooding or get to the surface!

There didn't appear to be any drawbacks to operating trimmed light when we were deep. So we did.

For several years, whenever we decided to go deep we pumped water out of the internal ballast tanks and kept the ship on the desired depth by ordering a down angle. The forces on the submarine were in equilibrium only when the ship was pointed six to ten degrees downward (so the power from the screw was pushing the ship down) to compensate for the upward buoyant force the surrounding water was exerting on the submarine.

After a few years, one ship discovered a definite downside to this practice.

First we must set the scene. There are normally three depth indicators available to the team of men controlling the ship's depth (called the diving party). One depth indicator displays depth digitally and directly in feet, like a car's odometer. In this example it would clearly show 364. The second depth indicator is a gauge with a needle that indicates the depth across a face inscribed in feet, and the mind has to extrapolate that the gauge is somewhere between the marks labeled 360 and 370. The last indication is a gauge that reads pressure in pounds per square inch. A reading of 44 psi is equivalent to 100 feet. If the gauge read 160 pounds, and you correctly divided by 44, you could determine that the ship was at 364 feet.

At the time of this incident, the procedure was that the ship's diving party would normally scan the first two gauges constantly (along with a couple of others), mentally comparing them, and occasionally look at the third pressure/depth gauge. People tend to find that 44 is not a convenient number by which to divide.

On the day of interest, while operating at a deep depth, the digtal-readout depth gauge on this ship stuck at a few feet shallower than the desired depth. As the submarine was not quite as light as the crew thought, the ship slowly drove itself deeper and deeper. No one recognized that the two other depth gauges were slowly creeping downward, correctly indicating that the ship was going deeper.

The ship went past its normal operating depth, past its safe depth, deeper, deeper than any submarine had ever gone before, ever deeper toward sure destruction.

A few feet short of catastrophe, someone looked at one of the ship's other depth indicators, noticed how deep they were, and ordered the submarine back up toward safety.

We almost lost this ship. What had gone wrong?

Several obvious things, but one was that humans and submarines normally operate on an even keel—or a "zero bubble" in submarine talk. The human's inner ear tells the body that level is good. We use this very sensitive sensor to walk, among other things. When we are off-level, even slightly, the ear complains and our body reacts.

By putting a deliberate down angle on the ship we had set up a condition the crew found completely artificial—foreign—abnormal.

Did that contribute to the people on the submarine overlooking the two other local depth indications that both clearly indicated the ship was deeper than was safe? Did that abnormality make it more difficult for the crew to recognize the pattern of hull-creaking as the increasing pressure of the increasing depth crushed the submarine ever smaller?

We thought so.

The crew certainly was distracted by something.

We made several changes in submarines as a result of this incident. For one thing, we don't trim light and run with a down bubble anymore. If the ship takes a down bubble now, except during the transitory conditions when the submarine is changing depth, then something is wrong. Now the inner ear, the brain, and the safe condition are all synchronized.

*    *    *

There is another common situation that appears to have a similar message.

Many of us have let a bedroom get into a state of disarray and subsequently found it impossible to locate something as simple as a shoe. When we finally find it, the shoe is often in plain sight, but is in a different location from the closet, or it's in the closet but on its side rather than flat on its sole, or arranged with the toe pointing out instead of sitting toe in and heel out, as our mind expected.

Whatever the mental mechanism that makes us overlook the shoe, experience says that permitting the twenty to fifty things in a bedroom to become disorganized makes it much, much harder to locate a missing shoe.

Imagine how impossible it is to find something wrong in the engine room of a cluttered and dirty submarine—which has tens of thousands of items! It is difficult enough to find what's wrong in the pattern when everything is spotlessly clean and every piece is in its own place.

So we submariners put a great deal of emphasis on keeping our submarines clean. It's not that we can tell the condition of some machine's bearings by looking at whether the turbine casing is neatly painted and free of all rust, corrosion, and oil. I can't. But I can't see anything wrong unless the object is first clean. Then, if it's also neat, my mind's eye looks around for less superficial aspects. I *may* then be able to see some indications of a developing problem.

We spend a lot of effort keeping submarines clean so they can tell us if they are working properly. If you want your workplace to whisper in your ear, substitute "factory" or whatever is your most challenging workplace for "submarine" in the above example.

People have difficulty in recognizing patterns when there are too many things wrong or when there is something too big that is wrong.* Both situations overtax the average person's recognition capability.

How does the good leader use this knowledge about patterns?

First, he seeks to build situations and systems so that differences

---

* This may be the reason people have such difficulty dealing with lack of integrity (a subject I shall discuss more directly later). When people are not honest about a situation, then it is difficult for others to deal with the subject because the patterns don't appear to run on grain.

in patterns will quickly show—so that he can manage by exception. The good leader recognizes that when the desired circumstances do not produce patterns, or result in patterns that are not readily recognizable, the problem not only demands more supervision but also cries out for new ideas.

Second, the good leader gets rid of distractors and keeps them away. He empties his workplace of unnecessary objects, dirt, and debris, as well as abnormal conditions. Only then has he properly prepared his environment for constructive work.

People work through some method of pattern recognition. Good leaders bend this trait into a management tool by eliminating unharmonious situations and establishing job patterns in which deviations will be obvious.

# CHAPTER SEVEN

## Change

Reduced to its basics, submarining is pretty simple. You want to keep the water out of the submarine and make the number of surfacings equal to the number of dives.

So why do submarines continue to require exceptional people to do such a simple job? Well, as the saying goes, the devil is in the details. A few examples always help. Let's review some basic things about submarines.

A submarine is a long pipe, about thirty to fifty feet in diameter, holding most of the machinery and all of the people. The arrangement of machinery inside the pipe, or hull, is not too different from what you may have seen in a surface ship.

The major difference in constructing a submarine (as compared to building a surface ship) is that the engineers can put more material inside the pipe of the submarine, for they don't have to worry about the submarine floating. In fact, for everything to work properly, the engineers want the pipe to weigh almost exactly as much as the water it displaces.

To control precisely when the ship will and will not float, ballast tanks are added wherever it is most convenient (usually on the ends or maybe wrapped around the bottom and sides). The principle is the same as tying water wings on a child swimmer. But, because the submarine wants to be able to submerge, there has to be an arrangement to let water displace the air inside the tanks. The tanks have permanent holes in the bottom of each tank, and valves at the top that can be used to start or stop the venting of each tank. The principle is the same as punching holes in the water wings. To save weight and mechanical complexity, there are no valves at the bottom, just gratings welded over the holes to keep larger fish from swimming in and taking up residence.

When the vents are opened and sea water is permitted to rise and completely fill the tanks, the whole ship weighs exactly as much as the sea water it displaces. The submarine is now neutrally buoyant and can steam along at the desired depth, without rising or falling, be it one or several hundred feet below the surface.

When the submarine decides to become a surface ship again, air is forced in the top of the ballast tanks (the vents were closed as soon as the ship was safely submerged). The air pressure forces the water out the bottom of the tanks through the permanently open gratings, and the submarine floats, held up again by metal-skinned water wings of air.

There are some other hardware details, but they are only peripheral to this discussion. Now for the tactics.

Up through two world wars, the submarine was essentially a surface raider that relied on its very low profile on the ocean to avoid detection. It submerged only to avoid aircraft or during the final attack phase against heavily armed warships (and, if the commanding officer was particularly audacious or the weather favored the submarine, sometimes not even then). Then, as now, when the submarine was below the surface of the water it was relatively invulnerable to all except fortunate attacks. On the surface it was a different story, for one direct hit on the submarine, be it by bomb or artillery round, was usually fatal.

When the submarine commander finally decided to submerge he wanted to do so quickly, for shot was often already on the way.

The quicker the submarine could dive and get completely below the surface of the water, the more margin it had for error. Thus the closer the submarine could approach a warship before slipping below the waves (where it was much slower and less capable), or the nearer it could permit an airplane to approach before diving to hide, the bigger the margin for error, the more kills made and the longer the submarine survived.

Submariners consequently wanted to dive fast and they wanted the first person who identified danger to be able to initiate the diving sequence. The men who were on the bridge of the submarine were the ones who had the best perspective and widest field of view. They thus normally sounded the diving alarm from the bridge.

What happened then?

When the blare of the diving alarm reverberated throughout the ship, men below decks instantly opened the large ballast vents and the ship started down. Simultaneously, the diesels were shut down and propulsion power shifted to the battery. Everyone on the ship raced to get the ship in its best watertight condition before water started pouring in.

Meanwhile the lookouts and officer of the deck were hustling down the ladders toward safety, stopping to shut the hatch to the bridge and, further down, the hatch to the access trunk. If they were too slow, if one of them slipped and fell in the dark or momentarily caught his clothing on one of the many projections in the sail, someone from inside the ship would reach up and shut the bottom hatch. The men from the bridge would be left to survive as best they could.

The trade-off at this point was the survival of the ship as compared to the lives of the men who sounded the alert.

Men who have served on diesel submarines all know of someone who was left, inadvertently or not, on the bridge or in the sail as the ship submerged beneath them.

By training and tradition, we ensured people will always choose the right answer—to leave their friends and shipmates behind. To make sure they didn't forget, during World War II the president gave the Medal of Honor to the widow of a commanding officer who directed his ship to submerge with him still on the bridge, injured.

When it happens in peacetime the ship resurfaces and looks for the man.

Often they find something.

There have also been ships lost with their entire crews during the diving sequence when one individual failed to close the right valves in the air induction system.

A dangerous business, but it is necessary to train the way we intend to fight. Unrealistic training is not valid training.

Now if you are or were a submariner, perhaps you got bored a page or two ago and skipped ahead to about here. You are now muttering to yourself, "Well, that is the way we used to do it. We had to do it that way for the good and valid reasons you have discussed. But with the advent of nuclear power, we no longer need air for combus-

tion engines and consequently submarines no longer have a reason ever
to be on the surface in unfriendly waters.

"In fact, our nuclear submarines normally now dive essentially as
soon as they leave port and remain submerged until they are ready to
come in port again. It is much, much safer to rig the ship completely
to dive, including having all the people down inside, and then slowly
dive the ship, carefully monitoring the manner in which the ship is
behaving, as well as all the machinery, pipes, and valves therein."
(Submariners sometimes talk to themselves this way.)

So say you.

And I say, that may be apparent to you today, but in 1970, aboard
the USS *Nautilus,* a full sixteen years after she had first gone to sea
powered by nuclear power, the crew was still diving that ship from
the bridge.

After getting this far in the chapter, I hope every reader will understand this was definitely dumb.

True. But some of the very best minds and men of our Navy and
submarine force had served or cycled through this particular ship. Why,
with all that talent, was the *Nautilus* still doing what was both tactically unnecessary and physically dangerous? Why hadn't anyone thought
of changing the diving procedure at the same time they were inventing a new war-fighting platform?

Beats me. But we didn't. Maybe we can think of some implica-
tions later.

Next story.

As you now understand how important it is that a submarine on
the surface be able to dive to escape danger, you can probably extrapolate that those aggressive World War II diesel submariners would
have figured out some way to ensure they could always get safely below
the surface, no matter what the material casualty.

Before we go any further, you need to know a little bit more about
the main ballast tank vents.

To submerge, remember, all that has to happen is for the air in
the ballast tanks to escape out the vents. So the ship's crew has to be
able to open the vents. The vents are located throughout the ship, but
are normally controlled from one central location, using hydraulic oil
pressure as the motive force.

Normally the vent valves are opened until the submarine's tanks
are fully under water, and then the valves are immediately reclosed.

Closing the vent valves is just as essential to submarine safety as opening them is essential to diving. They need to be closed in the event that something goes wrong—such as the ship being heavier than expected or another valve being in a wrong position—and the submarine starts to plunge instead of carefully sliding down.

Remember that the way the submarine surfaces is by pushing air into the ballast tanks to force water out the bottom. If the vent valves are still open when one tries to blow the water out, there is nothing to prevent the air from short-circuiting out the vents. If the air so escapes, the water remains in the ballast tanks. More importantly, but as part of the same physics equation, the submarine continues going deeper.

Enough facts. Story time.

Let us assume you were sitting in a diesel submarine on the surface in World War II and you had lost hydraulic power for some reason—and suddenly an airplane appeared over the horizon—what did you do? Well, you immediately executed what is known in our business as a hand dive.

To do a hand dive, teams went to the six to ten vents located high in the air in compartments throughout the ship. They climbed up in the overhead, isolated the hydraulic pressure so the valves could not be operated remotely (any sudden or unexpected return of pressure might cause the valve suddenly to spin open, breaking the sailor's arm), and cranked the valves open by hand. Meanwhile, other teams in the ship slowly hand-cranked the control planes and rudder to the desired angle.

I would wager that several diesel submarines were saved in World War II by the prompt and correct execution of this evolution. But . . .

. . . think what would happen if you were heavy in the forward part of the ship. Let's say you were twenty-five to fifty tons heavy. A lot for a diesel boat, but not unheard of for a nuclear one. And you opened the vents and pitched over and took a steep angle downward. And just one of the men who had opened the vent valves in the overhead fell away from his assigned valve and could not get back up to crank it *slowly* shut. Remember, to operate the valve by hand, the first step you took was to disable the ability to operate it remotely.

Right. You would probably all die.

Now, ask me why this is even interesting. We are on the verge of having a completely nuclear-powered submarine force. Why even talk about some old diesel boat procedures?

Well, we were doing hand dives aboard nuclear-powered ballistic missile submarines at least as late as 1968. We did them as drills. They were perfect score-breakers for inspections. Hell, we never would have done that for real. I mean, a ballistic missile submarine is never, never surfaced when it is on patrol. No nuclear submarine is. And a big ballistic missile submarine is very awkward while diving. Which is by design. There is no tactical reason to ever dive a nuclear submarine quickly.

I remember the last hand dive I did on a ballistic missile submarine. We were heavy forward.

Makes my stomach hurt to remember.

You think we were dumb to do it. Good call. But it was a "requirement" of the inspection we were undergoing. So we weren't the only dumb ones. For whatever solace that might have been later to my wife.

Oops, nearly forgot that I promised some words on the relevance of these particular stories. Here goes. Whatever your particular job, if it requires the exercise of leadership skills, then you are dealing with change. The fact that your job "used to be" very different is usually not evident. People often think that they are managing the same good way each day for the same good reasons. Not true! They or the job often change while no one is looking.

Each day's events alter something about your job. Usually the change is imperceptible. This is especially true for those closest to the events. Sometimes the change is not apparent over a long period, even if *radically* different organizational goals and processes have developed. I can assure you, however, that after disaster strikes, the fact that change had occurred will always be readily apparent to the investigative team.

How do you prevent calamity? The trick is to think consciously about why a particular something is done a particular way, and how that same something, or maybe even the larger "allthing," could be done more easily, with less risk, less expensively, or just better. More on this later. Now, on to the final story of this sequel.

Another discussion about diesel boats and those people who came next.

I know of only three things on board a submarine that can blow it to Kingdom Come. For the benefit of flatlanders, none of them is the reactor.

One is the oxygen system. A fire fed by pure oxygen is a roaring hell. A dieseled high-pressure air system is no picnic,* but the dieseling condition blows itself out and the ship will survive. An oxygen fire doesn't have the same manners. We never take shortcuts with any system involving oxygen.

The second is the explosion of a weapon aboard. Given the interlocks, it is probably the most unlikely of the three, but . . . it's there. Loading weapons is always serious business because of the potential forces available. An explosion as a result of a fire is also a remote possibility. Because the results would be so disastrous, whenever I walk a ship I always look for possible sources of fire near the weapons.

The third is the most likely culprit—the battery. The battery aboard a submarine is impressive. It is equivalent in size and energy to about a hundred thousand car batteries. It stores and dispenses a tremendous amount of energy on demand. It is one of those few systems aboard ship that are both operationally necessary and terribly, terribly dangerous.

While the battery is being fully charged up for use the chemical reaction that stores the energy produces hydrogen as a byproduct. A lot of hydrogen!

Humans breathe oxygen—so there are also literally tons of oxygen aboard a submarine.

Most of us have done that experiment in lab in which we put a very minute amount of hydrogen with an even smaller amount of oxygen and before we can even light a match—poof! A little water, a little heat, a little explosion.

If you did that experiment a lot of times, and filled your laboratory report sheet out carefully each time, you would determine that when the hydrogen level gets up to about eight percent of the whole mixture, it spontaneously combines with the oxygen in the air and gives

---

* A dieseling air system accident happens through the same principle used in a diesel-powered car. In both cases an air/oil mixture is suddenly pressurized. Some of the energy of the rapid pressurization turns to heat and ignites the oil. In a car engine, the oil or gasoline is deliberately introduced into a cylinder and the resultant energy smoothly propels the automobile down the road. In the high-pressure air system aboard ship the oil is there by mistake, and the explosion propels pieces of the system pell-mell throughout the compartment.

off a great deal of heat. In fact, it explodes. In the confined space of a submarine, the power of the explosion has proved to be sufficient to open up the steel of the hull faster than a King Kong can opener. That's right. Proved to be. We've done this. More than once on diesel boats.

So, to be safe aboard a submarine we always try to keep the hydrogen concentration below twenty-five percent of what will produce an explosion. Always have tried.

Aboard a diesel submarine, this was pretty easy. We charged the battery only when we were on the surface or at periscope depth running the diesels, so we could continuously flush the battery compartment with fresh air from outside the ship. The air that went through the battery well was then sucked into the big diesel intakes and quickly burned. The only problem occurred if somebody altered the position of the watertight doors and flappers (big valves for air) that shunted the air with the hydrogen back from the battery to the diesels. If this happened, we quickly had to stop charging the battery until we had figured out the problem. The submarine's crew had only seconds to react before the hydrogen concentration got sufficiently large to cause an explosion.

But this was usually not a problem. The battery was the only power source when the ship was submerged, and we normally did one or two battery charges a day. As a result, everybody aboard ship knew how important the battery was and what care it demanded. And even if people made mistakes, the system tended to be fail-safe—if the air flow to the diesels stopped, the diesels stopped. Without power, the battery charge stopped and hydrogen production stopped.

Yet, even with all of these things going for us—daily practice, everyone's acute awareness, and a fail-towards-safe system—accidents still occurred. Battery charging problems were always the most important single safety concern aboard a diesel submarine.

Now along came Admirals Rickover and Wilkinson and their invention of the nuclear submarine. Unlike diesels, a nuclear reactor did not need a supply of oxygen to produce power. So? How did that affect the battery?

Well, first, it meant that the battery was not used nearly as much. Aboard a diesel submarine the battery was the only source of power when the ship was submerged. Although they spent much of their time on the surface, diesel submarines normally dove at least once a day.

As one result, they used the battery at least once daily. Secondly, the battery was their only power source when the ship was submerged. Therefore, in order to keep their battery fully ready for possible tasking, the diesel submarine normally charged the battery at least daily.

As they did it all the time, and it was the most important evolution they did, the diesel submarine crew was very proficient in charging the battery and the attendant safety precautions.

On the other hand, aboard the nuclear submarine the nuclear reactor provided continuous motive power all the time—both while on the surface and when submerged. There suddenly was no routine and normal cyclic use of the battery. In fact, for several years some ships didn't charge their battery for months. Then, because inactivity is not good for a rechargeable battery, a technical decision was made to charge the battery at least every two weeks.

The more interesting (to this story) part of this change was that by preference the nuclear submarine under way at sea charged its battery when the ship was below periscope depth. It made sense. The nuclear submarine was a below-water animal. It was at its highest military efficiency if it adapted to operating away from the air/water interface. But there is only a finite atmosphere of air in the submarine. So we could no longer flush the battery compartment with air from the outside and then discard it overboard through the diesels.

Now, if we wanted to charge the battery while we were deep underwater, someone had to invent a machine that would harmlessly convert the hydrogen in the air to water.

Okay. Done. We called it the $CO/H_2$ burner.*

With one or two of these machines we could line up the air flow in the submarine so that it passed though these "burners" after picking up the hydrogen from the battery. We also had to change the procedures a bit** and modify the battery so it worked with the new pro-

---

* The machine also served another purpose by burning the deadly carbon monoxide (CO) to carbon dioxide. This conversion facilitated another machine's use of a chemical reaction to remove the carbon dioxide from the air. The chemical reaction wouldn't work with carbon monoxide, necessitating the conversion step.
** Because a higher charging rate makes more hydrogen, especially near the end of the evolution, we reduced the rate at which we charged the battery at the finish, and the manner in which we made sure the battery was fully topped off.

cedures. In the end, we had more hydrogen in the ship than previously, when it was all being dumped overboard, but it was still below the safe level.

Time for another slight technical diversion. You need to know a little bit about the procedure a submarine uses for coming to periscope depth.

When the submarine comes to periscope depth it has to sort out what is happening on the surface—without actually being able to see anything. And right before coming up the submarine has to work through a mixed-up layer of a hundred or so feet of water near the surface. This is the exact same mixed-up water that makes antisubmarine warfare so difficult for surface ships.

Coming to periscope depth, especially several years ago, was like a blind man walking into an unfamiliar living room and making his way to the kitchen—without bumping into anything.

Some of us are quite good at it.

But it remains one of the most difficult evolutions a submarine performs. Most commanding officers, who nightly sleep peacefully and trust their officer of the deck with the lives of everyone aboard, still manage to wander out to the control room and watch each or nearly each trip to periscope depth.

When a diesel boat was coming to periscope depth it set what was called Condition Baker. This evolution shut all the doors and hatches and placed the ship in its most watertight condition. The theory was that if something were to go wrong and the submarine were rammed by a surface ship the only people who would die would be those who were unfortunate enough to be in the affected compartment.

Good, conservative policy. Like nearly everything else that seemed prudent, we incorporated that policy directly into our nuclear submarine operating procedures.

And probably inadvertently set the stage for the loss of a submarine a decade later.

Picture this. The submarine is under way, submerged, conducting a battery charge. We do a battery charge only about every two weeks instead of daily, so it is no longer routine. As it isn't routine everyone isn't always thinking about the procedures to carry out in the event of an abnormal condition. We have been conducting the battery charge for several hours, and are almost at the end—which happens to be exactly the time when hydrogen is generated most profusely. Not a problem.

Everything is carefully balanced. We have the ship's ventilation system lined up for maximum air flow. Air is passing through the forward watertight doors back through the engine room flappers, into the engine room and the two $CO/H_2$ burners, back through the flappers to the battery compartment. . . .

Time to go to periscope depth.

"Set Condition Baker throughout the boat."

Everywhere in the ship, people leap to shut the watertight doors and flappers to place the ship in a safer condition to come to periscope depth. In the engineering area someone notes that the air flow has dropped. No problem. The reactor doesn't need air to operate.

Suddenly: "Look at the hydrogen level in the battery compartment! It's skyrocketing! Stop the charge!"

Too late.

Poof.

When nuclear-powered submarines incorporated Condition Baker into their procedures, we didn't think about the effect of this routine procedure on the battery charge.*

We lost the USS *Scorpion* at sea for unknown reasons about thirty years ago. Some people think it was lost as a result of a battery explosion. Not terribly surprising when you think about the scenario we created by setting Condition Baker aboard nuclear ships. The last time I was aboard a submarine that set Condition Baker, or its modern equivalent, was less than ten years ago. The crew thought they were being conservative. Maybe.

Or maybe they had never actually thought about it.

This chapter is titled "Change." Why, and why these particular three stories?

First, when I review the transition the United States Navy has undergone in my professional lifetime in shifting from diesel to nuclear submarines, I am surprised how, at any one time you care to select

---

* Eventually we recognized that any value of setting Condition Baker aboard most nuclear submarines had been negated because we had gone to fewer and larger compartments on a submarine. Flooding any compartment was going to result in the loss of the entire ship.

during that transition, the people I ran around with consistently underestimated the significance and immensity of that change. We just never sat down and fully thought through the ramifications of the submarine changing from a low-visibility, low-profile World War II commerce raider to its position as the stealthy queen of the oceans.

Because the same officers and crew proceeded from diesel submarines directly over to nuclear ones, we did not recognize that the submarine had gone from a limited-capability surface ship to an underwater platform more powerful than any in Jules Verne's most improbable dreams. If we had stopped to consider, we might have realized that nuclear submarines were a radically new warfare platform.

Thinking of them only as an incremental improvement got us in trouble. We would have been better off if we had sat down immediately and reexamined every last one of the operational axioms the submarine force had passed down from its first fifty years.

In our new true submarines, some of the old axioms were invitations to death.

In this chapter I have discussed three operating practices that used to be common practice in submarines. In each case, those of us involved finally figured out that the procedures were not only not the best ones for nuclear submarines, they were potentially dead wrong. I feel sure we haven't yet found them all.*

Why haven't we? Perhaps Aristotle, or some other great independent thinker, if given the concept of a true underwater vehicle, and a proper statement of what was desired (to recharge a battery safely, or to submerge to become stealthy, or whatever), might have recognized that a new nuclear vehicle demanded dramatically different procedures. But that isn't the way we less-brilliant humans work. We like continuity. Most of us are comfortable with patterns. Comfortable with identifiable sameness. We have trouble adapting to change. We have difficulty recognizing when there is a need for change.

---

* For example, even though a submarine's bridge is unprotected and low in the water, and every year or so we lose men when an unexpectedly large wave washes over, some commanding officers do not require everyone on the bridge or sail at sea to wear a safety harness hooked to a retainer on the bridge. You didn't do it on a diesel boat because the safety of the ship dictated that you be able to get off the bridge immediately—you couldn't chance hanging up on a clumsy harness. Commanders don't do it on a nuclear submarine because—?

As a result, change is one of the most important products in any organization. And those individuals who can recognize when there is a need for change, or identify what that change should be, are among the most valuable individuals in any organization. Lots of people can make something incrementally better. Only the extraordinary individual makes change happen.

So what if you want to be that extraordinary individual? How do you start?

One way is to be alert to the bumps.

When something does not quite go wrong enough to cause a problem, but still prevents or hampers a perfectly smooth event, do you proceed blithely on, or do you return to that bump and make sure you understand what caused it? Often, you don't have to stop the train or turn everybody around, you just have to make sure you mark the location of the bump in your mind and don't clear it from that computer under your hair until you have solved the problem to your satisfaction. You may not have enough data at the moment. You may have to do months of investigation, thinking, and evaluation. But don't let it go until you understand it. There is always a dirty reason lying underneath a bump.

Another facilitator to change is always to be trying to reevaluate whether what you are doing still makes sense. Your goals change frequently. You learn new things. Do you change your habits as a result? Don't be one of life's passenger pigeons. Pick up everything that isn't bolted down and look for the reason for change that may be growing there.

Recognizing, understanding, and making things change is the wellspring of any successful organization—including our country's submarine force.

Next subject.

# CHAPTER EIGHT

## Admission

I hate hats.

Can't stand them. No matter how large a hat I buy, after about half an hour resting atop my head the band starts creeping inward until soon my forehead is captured in a viselike grip. I inevitably get a headache if I wear a hat for very long. Unfortunately, my business requires such an accessory. I enjoy the leadership opportunities, excitement, and challenges my particular business provides, so I ignore the headaches. They are not so bad if I don't think about them.

Whether it was a subconscious choice or not, I ended up in submarines. No one has to wear a hat aboard a submarine. Submarines have always approached this differently than the surface ship community, where everyone stands around under a roof with hats on. Remember all those World War II movies? I have served aboard surface ships. They are correct. The sun and rain don't often get in the eyes of people who wear hats indoors.

When I began living and working on submarines, very few people even wore a complete uniform under way. Aboard submarines there was no heating or air conditioning, and no water for showers. The air temperatures varied between 25° and 120°F both day and night, and no one ever complained about anyone else's body odor. You wore shorts and shower shoes during the summer, and everything you had aboard, including the Christmas sweater from Aunt Mildred, during the winter. Practicality was the only watchword for dress.

Then we ruined it all by inventing nuclear submarines, which had sufficient power to run air conditioning plants in the summer and to power electric heaters during the winter.

It was amazing to me how quickly the submarine force reverted to middle-of-the-road conformity. Five years after I had been used to wearing shorts and shower shoes aboard diesel submarines, I was aboard a nuclear submarine under way, submerged on a long patrol, and the executive officer announced that "tie and jacket" would be the required wear for evening meals. Let's see . . . I am working eighteen hours a day, seven days a week, sleeping four hours each day with only an hour or two left for eating and relaxing, and now I am supposed to do that in a tie and jacket. Hell, I don't even have a tie with me. No problem for the executive officer. He isn't working his tail off. He often takes a nap in the afternoon. The evening meal is his big event of the day.

Fortunately, in the relatively dim light of a submarine, four black socks knotted together looked a lot like a black tie. Or at least the combination looked sufficiently regulation to get us both through the last two months of that patrol. I have met only one executive officer like that.

About the same time, Admiral Zumwalt took over the helm of the Navy. He established several new policies which in general were wildly popular with the junior people (officer and enlisted), and not nearly so well supported by the officers and enlisted men who had been around for a while. One example fits particularly well the point I will eventually make.

First you have to know that an officer's working uniform aboard ship is those khakis you all have seen, while the enlisted working uniform is a denim shirt and trousers called dungarees (which look a lot like jeans). You also ought to realize that those ice cream whites the public likes to see were never intended for work, but are definitely intended to make a ship and crew look impressive to the natives of Bora Bora.

There is not one ounce of practicality involved in either the enlisted or officer white uniforms. Those white billboards not only pick up dirt, but attract even the pollen in the air. "Whites" have to be cleaned every time they are worn, even if you slipped them on for only an hour. In addition (especially with the fabrics in use at the time of this story) whites have to be dry-cleaned and thus are very expensive to keep up.

Enough background. Back to the story. The Navy policy at the time was that enlisted men who lived off base could not wear their working uniform to and from work. Let's assume it's summer and a man is assigned to a submarine. He leaves home wearing his whites, drives in, and changes to dungarees. He then works hard all day, disassembling and reworking engines, perhaps taking a break to paint for a while, maybe crawling under an oily foundation to look at a trouble area. He spends the last half hour on his hands and knees cleaning up his work area. At the end of his work day he is sweaty, dirty, paint- and oil-stained—just like most of the other men aboard.

Oops. Forgot to tell you. There is only one shower aboard ship for about every thirty to forty men (even assuming no one is doing maintenance work on some part of the shower system).

So the men wash their hands and comb their hair, and climb back into those lovely whites for the drive home. By the time each man gets home his whites are filthy on the inside and wrinkled on the outside. Time to get a set of whites dry-cleaned again.

Right, I agree it was a stupid policy (especially as officers were permitted to wear their working uniform, khakis, to and from work). Admiral Zumwalt agreed it was stupid. He changed the policy to permit men to wear their working uniforms to and from work. He added the limitation that men wearing a working uniform had to minimize their contact with the public (don't wear dirty dungarees downtown after work to go shopping for a new suit).

Unfortunately, one of the five hundred thousand men and women in the Navy wandered into a bar in Norfolk one evening after work in dirty dungarees and, several hours later, was arrested for being drunk in public. His commanding officer somehow felt that the picture his man presented by lying drunk on the street in nondescript dungarees was immeasurably worse than it would have been if the body had been dressed in Navy whites. So the commanding officer felt embarrassed and pointed out to his boss (and everyone else in the Navy) that he (the commanding officer) could not be held responsible for keeping discipline aboard his ship if Admiral Zumwalt hamstrung him by letting obviously irresponsible people wear dungarees.

I know it sounds stupid.

But this happened precisely the way I have related.

In fact, this whole issue became a cause célèbre and the forces of darkness eventually won.* The policy permitting enlisted men and women to wear working clothes during their daily travel to and from the ship was rescinded.**

These little stories are interesting, "But what is your point?" you may be saying. Well, to begin with, this chapter is intended for young men and women who are starting their careers. Let me assure you that it doesn't matter which field you are entering, it is an absolutely cinch bet that you are going to work for people who are going to give you ample reason to quit.

You are going to work for people who don't care about people, don't understand people, and are apparently willing to go out of their way to make your life, as well as that of your friends, an imbroglio.

There is also going to be at least one, and probably many more, difficult aspects to your intended career. Your career is either going to involve early hours (you have always been a night person), require a clean shaven and conservatively suited appearance (you have worn a beard since it was but a blond wisp on your cheeks, and you wore an open-neck shirt to your prom), or require you to work with people who believe Hester Prynne got exactly what she deserved.

Nevertheless, do not lose sight of your goal. If it is to win fame and glory, or even to make the best use of your talents, you must take on the most difficult challenges, compete with the most competent peo-

---

* Good doesn't have any unique advantages. Usually it relies on the quality and quantity of its supporters here on Earth. In this case, Admiral Zumwalt needed the votes of men who didn't understand the concept of caring about people (the Navy is not an autocracy), and he had to give way here to retain the progress he had made on other issues.

** The compromise reached permitted enlisted men to wear civilian clothes, rather than whites, to and from work. Of course, this meant that they were getting their own clothes filthy every night they went home. The only people who weren't unnecessarily ruining clothes were those men and women who weren't working, or those blue-collar men who were in cushy nonengineering jobs. And the compromise didn't apply to everyone. It was labeled a "benefit," and applied only after the individual had spent a year or two in the Navy and moved up the advancement ladder a bit. Of course, the more junior people do the most dirty work, so if one is truly interested in people . . . . It was a terrible compromise. It encouraged people not to work hard and adversely affected the new employees who were so difficult to recruit and retain.

ple, and play in the big leagues. Whatever your big league, I will tell you now that it is going to have rules with which you will disagree. There are two things to remember:

1. The rules are made, and changed, by those at the top. You won't even get near the top unless you start, stay with it, and keep at it.

2. If you truly want the benefits of some particular career success, treat your job with at least the same seriousness you would if you were dying to see a particular movie. Wishing doesn't do it. Doesn't matter how much you want to see that movie, doesn't matter if Natalie is acting out your own life story right there on the screen—if you really want to see that movie, the most certain way to ensure you get inside is to pay the price of admission.

I think of this every time I put on my hat.

# CHAPTER NINE

## Assignments

The most important policies in many organizations concern how and where people are assigned. Every employee is interested in where he is going to live, as well as what his new job will be.

These are not just "people issues" that can safely be ignored. People issues almost inevitably involve significant organizational principles. In the submarine force, and I suspect elsewhere, personnel assignment practices and policies often have unexpected results. Some results are serendipitous. Some are not.

Once upon a time there was a nuclear submarine that was simply doing everything wrong. She was very costly to maintain. She never went to sea. She was like an expensive mistress with a migraine condition. She had managed to stretch an overhaul until its duration was counted in years instead of months. Then, during her first at-sea exercise period following that overhaul she had come up underneath an aircraft carrier, and subsequently spent long months in a second shipyard trying to unbend the sail. Next she had been sent for ninety days to a third shipyard, and repairs there had dragged on for fifteen long months.

This particular submarine had been to sea only eight days in the past seven years, so she hadn't done anything useful for anybody for a long time. (Unless you have Air Force leanings and count hitting the carrier as a plus.) Her material condition was still a mess, morale was nowhere, and the submarine was the laughingstock of the waterfront.

So the people who do this sort of thing selected a good officer and ordered him into a key billet on that submarine and waited for it all to get better. It didn't. Maybe conditions weren't going downhill quite as fast, but they surely hadn't started swinging up.

So the Navy personnel people picked another good officer and sent him into the fray.

And in the next few months we replaced nearly every officer and senior enlisted man on that ship with specially selected individuals. And we spent more money and got more supervisors involved. Finally we established a pace such that everybody on board was working an *average* of more than sixteen hours a day, seven days a week.

After more than a year of this we finally got the ship up to below average. Which had been a long climb!

We never totalled the financial costs. The cost in people was about twenty-five officers who resigned either in disgust or exhaustion and two hundred enlisted men who opted out for similar reasons. About half of those who left were fine people any organization would like to keep. One later became an assistant secretary of the Navy. Several became lawyers (your choice as to which half you think the lawyers were in).

After going through a situation like that, for a long time you are sure of only one thing—you don't want to do it again. Then, when you finally have time to breathe, a second question begins to edge into your mind at night—what was the cause?

It turns out we don't normally do a postmortem on the really big mistakes that stretch on for years. Possibly a review would be too tough. On the other hand, maybe too many people become involved in a problem that goes on for that long. The more people involved, the greater the likelihood that at least one is still around who would just as soon not publicly exhume the corpse. Probably wouldn't learn anything anyway—a similar situation won't ever come up again.

It does make it awfully difficult to identify exactly what not to do again. Tough for the younger men and women to learn what they should avoid. Too bad.

Well, if you are really interested, here is how I remember it.

Each officer who has come into the nuclear submarine force has gone through about a year of theoretical and practical engineering training to learn how to operate a nuclear reactor safely. Then each has done some additional classroom training in the operation and control of submarines.

This is not just idle training. Admiral Rickover believed that people need to challenge themselves in order to grow—but that in our current education system too many of the very brightest only skim along, not working very hard. The brightest always do well for what he felt was the poorest of reasons—simply because they are smarter than everyone else.

All of us have been in groups where there were one or two individuals who got terrific grades without working very hard. Certainly they weren't working as hard as we were, and they were still doing better. Admiral Rickover believed those people were America's most underdeveloped resource. He felt his personal life was an example of what an average intellect, if he only worked hard, could accomplish. If the superstars would only work as he did, think what they could accomplish for the country!

Admiral Rickover believed in America, as well as the potential of nuclear power, and he believed that America needed our superstars' genius. Throughout his life he did his best to motivate men and women who had such potential.

As one result, Admiral Rickover worked hard to develop highly visible carrots and sticks for each of his training programs. The problem was, it was always difficult to grow good carrots. It was easy to find sticks to threaten laggards. But that wasn't Rickover's goal. His real interest was finding the right buttons for young people. How was he going to enthuse the individuals who had gotten straight As all their lives without really working?*

A method he used for years was to base the student's next geographical assignment on his class standing. There were nuclear reac-

---

* Admiral Rickover was willing to try about anything. One of the more interesting attempts was to give everyone a lengthy examination the first day of class (the exam adjusted for differences in the quality of the college they had attended or their particular college grading system). The second day, people with the top twenty scores were in one room, the next twenty in the second, the next twenty in the third room, etc. Sounds like a normal track system, doesn't it? The only difference was that the grading system was a bell curve for each class (the same seventy-eight percent score could be a B in the lowest room and an F in the top class) and it was announced that twenty-five percent from each class would fail and be dropped from the program!

It didn't work. The valedictorians from Berkeley and the Naval Academy blew the bell curve in the top class high and left. All the other eighteen would have failed. Instead, pragmatism won and the two of them were redistributed down into the lowest class.

tor prototypes, which we were using as training platforms, located in the East (Connecticut) and the West (Idaho). Some men liked the big cities and the sophistication of the East. Others liked the informality and the outdoor activities of the West. Many had girl friends on one particular side of the country. Sports and sex—a young man's carrots.

So, in Admiral Rickover's program, the assignment to the next training site was based upon class standing. If you stood first, you chose first, second, you chose second, and so on until all but one training site was filled, and then the pack was wedged into what was left. To make it even more interesting, only the top half of each class chose in order. If you were in the bottom half, you had to enter a lottery to determine your order of selection. Thus, in a forty-person class, if you stood twenty-first it was possible that you would get what was left.

As only about the top ten percent of any class couldn't be bumped into the bottom half by about a week of extra effort by those in the middle, this arrangement ensured that most of the entire class would always be working.

I don't know of any problems this ever caused in the training commands. Doesn't seem that it should have—trainees don't have much more responsibility than keeping track of their lunch boxes.

However, all things must end, even school, and eventually everyone got to the end of the training pipeline. For most people, the last stop was Submarine School in New London, Connecticut. Here the selection of the first duty station was made the same way school sites had been chosen.*

Seemed like a reasonable policy. It meant that the people in Washington actually responsible for making assignments got fewer telephone calls from people wanting to influence that decision. It meant that the admiral's son didn't automatically get a submarine out of San Diego (probably our most desirable home port). Fair is fair. We selected by class standing for years. The danger was so insidious that no one saw it coiling.

---

* One could well argue that Admiral Rickover would not have made the mistake of continuing this policy to assignments to nontraining commands. But he didn't have any influence over Submarine School assignment policy at this time. He did later, partially as a result of the events I am describing, but that gets a little ahead of this story.

Just a little more background. In the submarine force there is a distinct pecking order in the desirability of ships, driven largely by the average number of medals that can be earned and the particular exotic reputation of foreign ports the ship visits. This is not because danger and travel are everyone's cup of tea. Some of the men in submarines are family men who enjoy a white picket fence as much as the next fellow—and get a great deal of pleasure from mowing neatly trimmed lawns, as well as having barbecues with the wife, neighbors, children, and the dog.

But they don't talk about it.

The submarine force is like any other group of young men bursting with ego and testosterone. Most know they will live forever, so danger is to be sought. Most also know that life is short (they have been living only since they left home after high school), so foreign travel must be done now, before the world ends and the Grateful Dead quit giving concerts.

Therefore it is very, very in to want to be aboard attack submarines that are deploying to Hong Kong, Bangkok, and Singapore, or Cannes, Naples, and Stockholm. It is less interesting to be aboard ballistic missile submarines in Charleston or Georgia, but at least ballistic missile submarines go to sea, where danger lurks beneath every wave.

It is absolutely uninteresting to be aboard a submarine in overhaul, which, besides being hard work, appears to provide little or no chance to be a warrior. But—if that submarine is going to get out of overhaul soon and then make exotic port calls—maybe that's okay.

It is absolutely horrible to be aboard a ballistic missile submarine in overhaul, because, even when it gets out of dock, it still isn't going anywhere very interesting.

With the understanding that the peer group will not understand selection of anything other than the saltiest attack submarine (unless someone is engaged to a someone who has a unique disease that requires treatment by one doctor who is stationed in the one hospital located in Kings Bay, Georgia, an excuse that can be easily overused), it is easy to predict exactly the order in which submarine assignments will be selected. And that's precisely what happened for years.

There was one other group of submarines that was even less attractive than ballistic missile submarines in overhaul. When Admiral Rickover and his group invented submarines, they did what today would be called "fly-before-buy." They actually spent about a decade building several different designs and running them around the ocean while deciding what worked best and what didn't work at all. These submarines were the fleet's new toys and were at sea practically every day of the year. They had very little time off-line for maintenance. As the old horseman's expression goes, these submarines were "run hard and put away wet."

Once the decision had been made on a group of desirable operational characteristics, the design was more or less frozen and a group (or class) of submarines was built with every effort expended to make the class as good as possible. The early one-of-a-kinds were rapidly shunted to the back of the bus. They were no longer the wave of the future. Any one of the new class was generally better tactically than the best of the one-of-a-kinds.* In addition, the one-of-a-kinds were truly that, and keeping them running was difficult. Factories that made wooden gimcracks burned down and now gimcracks had to be made by hand—and it took six months. Not a big problem to the submarine force. Only one submarine had ever used wooden gimcracks. Somewhat of a problem to that particular submarine. They had to learn how to make gimcracks themselves.

As you might suspect, after a decade or so the submarines that were one-of-a-kind had the reputation of not operating too much and being even harder to keep running. An accurate assessment. One even the greenest recruit could make.

And did.

It wasn't long before all of the one-of-a-kinds were filled with people who had stood in the bottom half of their Submarine School class. When these one-of-a-kinds had been commissioned they had been filled to the very brim with exceptional experienced officers—the very best the Navy could offer! Now the best officer aboard was below average.

And because these ships were so difficult and one-of-a-kind, we decided that we should have the same officer do successive tours on the same ship, for the one-of-a-kinds were hard to learn. So a particular officer would serve as a division officer, and after three or four years move up to be a department head on the same ship, and then

---

* For those interested, I am lumping the *Nautilus, Seawolf, Triton,* and *Tullibee,* and the *Skate* and *Skipjack* classes into my "one-of-a-kind" category, and saying that the first class was the thirteen-ship 594 or *Permit* class.

after another three years perhaps be executive officer on the same ship. Sometimes an officer selected to be commanding officer was ordered back to a particular ship on which he had served previous tours. He knew the ship and had done an excellent job there. Seemed like a good idea.

It wasn't.

It was the late sixties before the submarine organization fully realized that nearly every one-of-a-kind was in serious trouble. It was a couple of years more before everyone comprehended how hard it was going to be to make them better. It was nearly half a decade more before all were well.

There were probably several reasons the one-of-a-kinds got into trouble. Maybe more. But there were only two things we changed to fix the problem. So let's consider those two.

First we stopped the policy of assigning people to repeat tours in the same command. Like a crushed car, it had several bad angles. One is that it seems nearly everybody acquires a certain number of wrong ideas. If they stay in one command and gradually grow more senior, their wrong ideas are often never corrected. On the other hand, if they go to another command incorrect ideas are usually challenged by the first person who hears them. The normal "new guy" treatment serves to uncover and eliminate misconceptions and bad ideas.

A second problem with repeat tours is that everyone learns a certain amount at each command and then appears to stagnate. Might as well sit down and kick back, he already knows it all. Let's say that the first person who comes aboard a submarine is a superstar and learns ninety percent of what there is to know about the ship. Then he moves up to the next level, where he learns only about thirty percent of what he should. Or it may work out that he expects new officers to learn only ninety percent of what he did, which is actually only eighty-one percent of what there is to know. Whatever the mechanism, if people are ordered back to the same command or left there the knowledge level of the group quickly drops off. The impact looks like some sort of horrible mathematical regression at work. Whatever is happening, it is not good.

The third bad angle to repeat tours is that they make it harder for the organization to improve. Management in all organizations, and this is especially true of the submarine force, is continually trying to raise performance and standards. Turnover of people in particular units is especially effective on facilitating changing standards. If you leave the same people in the same unit they will remember that a certain level of performance was satisfactory last year, and they will (perhaps unconsciously) work toward that level, rather than toward the new higher standard the organization wishes to establish.

In addition, if the crew tried to meet higher goals and failed before, its members "know" they can't do it. New people don't have these old negative facts. In this case, ignorance is often bliss and success may come quickly.

Finally, the routine and frequent rotation of people between units speeds up the spread of the information just like a basketball crowd quickly spreads a winter virus. Organizations routinely have difficulty effectively passing new knowledge along to everyone or even encouraging applications of a new idea. Given the impediments to information transfer that exist, the informal conversations of new individuals in new commands often turn out to be one of our most effective new idea distribution networks.*

I said there were two things we did to fix the problem on the one-of-a-kinds. The first was to stop rotating people back to the same submarines, and no longer to permit someone to move up to the next senior job in the same submarine. The second fix we made was to stop the practice of letting young officers select their own first assignment out of Submarine School.

We had foolishly set ourselves up a system by which the less capable officers went to the harder jobs. In fact, we had managed to establish wardrooms in which all of the officers aboard were academically below average! Doesn't mean all the officers weren't nice guys. Many were. Doesn't mean that some of them were not the best all-around offi-

---

* The senior manager often disrupts this natural process by amassing a personal staff or group of sycophants and taking them with him from job to job. Taking along such personnel baggage ensures that the senior manager will never look at the new job with equally new eyes, and may make it impossible for him to adapt quickly to new responsibility. It ensures he drags his prejudices and former opinions into a new arena. In addition, the very existence of these "old" people on "new" staffs ensures that the rest of the staff believe the new manager is not interested in their opinions, and ensures that the old friends will have a disproportionate bureaucratic weight in the new organization, no matter where they are actually placed (or their competence in this new field).

cers. Some were. But if you have a tough job do you want your best achievers trying to do it? Of course you do.

But if I can't award the easy jobs to the better executives, then how do I ever reward the achievers, you say? And I answer, don't sweat it. If success is not its own reward for achievers—who wants them?

The nicest thing I can say about someone is that he or she always asks for the toughest jobs. We all are only on this earth for a limited time. If someone is a major league player he doesn't want to waste his time hitting home runs against minor league pitching. If he's just interested in padding his slugging average he isn't major league. Trade him.

We fixed the problem in submarines in the sixties. In fact, we even started especially detailing particularly good senior officers to these one-of-a-kind ships to ensure the better officers got the tougher jobs.

Hard problem to keep fixed. People inevitably think they know best what their next job should be. People forget that jobs change dramatically in value depending on the needs of the organization at that particular time. Some people waste lots of time scheming to get particular jobs. And when they are successful they usually have managed to get their square little body right smack into a round hole. Spend your time working instead. Then maybe you will deserve a tougher job. Which you won't want. And if you do it well, maybe somebody will give you a tougher one. Which you also won't want. If you keep your mouth shut and keep working, you may look around some day and find yourself considered a success. One thing for sure, you won't have gotten there by hitting minor league pitching.

To sum up this story, the problem with our particular unit was that our parent organization had assigned a group of average people to do probably the toughest job in the submarine force. Then, to ensure the task was impossible, they had retoured them on the same unit. We fixed the problem in the end by firing all the average guys, assigning a bunch of our best officers and enlisted men to the ship, and working their collective butts off literally for years.

The larger good of the organization is sometimes not particularly interesting, understood, or even visible at that level. The average guys had their self-images damaged. They believed they had failed and left the Navy in disappointment. The better young officers just thought the Navy was screwed up. The results were the same. Most of them also left.

# CHAPTER TEN

## Limits

I believe that leadership is a wonder drug for any organization. At the same time, we have all seen occasions when leadership was not enough. Why? How can you recognize such situations? What do you do when you face one?

I have already discussed one time leadership wasn't enough. In the "Assignments" chapter I remarked that despite assigning some of our better leaders to the older submarines, we found it wasn't enough. The submarine force didn't start to lick the one-of-a-kind problem until we altered some basic personnel assignment policies. We had to decide to spend our "personnel wealth" on those ships. That eventually worked.

There is a footnote to that story. For the next decade, every time we decided we could finally get by without putting a disproportionate share of our personnel assets into those particular submarines, each one-of-a-kind would immediately start to wobble like the last plate on a juggler's row of spinning reeds. We would quickly have to return to ordering in our best people.

Okay, that's an example. We have considered that one. I know another.

Now, this story contains a lot of sidetracks. I have left them in deliberately. They are like events commemorated by state historical markers: perhaps not significant enough for national recognition, or their own chapters in a book, but quite deserving of individual signposts. Some of them may be hard to read if you are just whizzing through. Please slow down and get full value from each.

This particular story started one day when the Navy inspector general reported there were problems on a submarine operating base, problems similar to the ones he had also noted the previous year.

If you are not familiar with the inspector general concept, it is a simple one. Large commands or companies with widespread forces need to have someone who routinely travels everywhere to probe for unreported problems.

Sometimes the inspector general visits an area to investigate a known problem. More often he acts as an unbiased, listening ear to ensure that the guy at the top is getting accurate reports. The inspector general also checks to ensure someone follows up and takes action on those things in which the organization's big boss is particularly interested.

As one facet of his job, every year the inspector general visits each Navy area, sets up shop somewhere out of the way, and invites people to come talk to him if they have specific or general complaints.

Most of the time the silence is deafening.

There shouldn't be anything there to hear. When he sees something wrong, a person ought to report it to his supervisor. People shouldn't wait for some unknown inspector general to come to town.

When problems get reported as they occur, they get solved as they occur. It's like maintaining any complex piece of machinery. If you work every day at fixing what's wrong, you don't wake up some morning simply overwhelmed with broken equipment. Same thing with people. If you work each day at solving your personnel problems, you never quite seem to build up a critical mass of unhappy people.

On the other hand, some places always seem to be having people problems.

They are the same places where reported wrongs don't generate visible reaction.

People don't feel they are taken seriously there. The command doesn't devote efforts to solving the problem, or, if the problem isn't a real one, doesn't try to change perceptions. Instead, people feel they are always getting brushed off.

It can get worse. In commands where the boss doesn't have enough experience or self-confidence, sometimes the command practices a policy of "shooting the messenger." Reporting bad news in one of these commands immediately ensures the reporter is given some of the blame for the problem—any problem.

People aren't dumb. It isn't too long before information stops walking through the doorway in those commands.

It can even get worse. Sometimes a supervisor gets the bright idea of intimidating the complainer.

Terrific idea. Now instead of finding out what people are worried about and exposing their concerns to the healing sunlight, the intimidators make sure both the people and the problems fester. It will work for a while. Intimidation always seems to work at least long enough to ensure there will be plenty of pus when the sore is finally poked.

When a stranger with authority rides into an intimidated town, and— with the promise of anonymity—inquires about injustice, people seem to rise right up out of the sagebrush. Each one knows about the most interesting problem!

Now the command has to solve the problems on the inspector general's time schedule. And now it doesn't even get to know where the fire started.

Makes it a hell of a lot harder to find out what's really going on.

Stop for a moment and think about three basic rules for any leader to remember *always*:

—review every reported wrong.
—never kill the messenger.
—intimidation is dumb.

Back to our story. The previous year, we had received a series of complaints about the way in which a particular base was operated. An inspection was done.* Some things were fixed. The consensus was that

---

* The investigation team was headed up by another submarine base commanding officer. Seemed reasonable. He should have had the right cognitive base. There was one small flaw in this appointment. Although it was not realized at the time, the chief investigator had the same personal problem (he drank a bit too much) as the people he was investigating. Not surprisingly, the investigation report concluded there were no major problems. Nevertheless, not all the team members agreed. We tend to think of the military as an autocratic organization. It often is. But truth and justice usually prevail. One of the team members discussed his reservations with a friend, and shared documents and opinions that had not made it into the final report. A year later, the person with whom he shared his thoughts was on the team that reinvestigated the same base.

You can't and shouldn't paper over problems. The smell will eventually seep out. Doing what's right the first time, no matter how painful, is the only policy that will stand the test of time.

the old commanding officer was the cause of much of the unrest.* A new guy was ordered in. A year later the same inspector general came into town. This year, last year's complainers had kept diaries. Detailed diaries.

Complainers often have no sense of perspective. They are unhappy and want everyone else to be the same. They go out of their way to look for company policies and actions to find objectionable. They appoint themselves as the command's whistle-blower. They report everything as wrong.

One of the most difficult parts of any investigation in this situation is determining what is important. You can't throw out even the most minor complaint without first reviewing it to ensure it doesn't help confirm a bigger problem. The investigator has to keep his own sense of perspective. He can't become emotional. He has to ensure he picks each of the items up, looks it over carefully, understands what it is and what effect it has, and puts it away in its own little box. When the good investigator is through the scene has to look, as well as be, impeccably clean.

The individuals keeping the diaries had written down every rumor they heard. Some of the reported facts contradicted others. Some of the reported incidents were obviously false. Others were slanderous. Some were purely malicious. It was like a history of the Hatfields written by the McCoys. You had to understand the relationships to sort out the probable slant. A couple of the accusations caught people's attention. One was that the submarine force was disguising a serious drug problem.

Were we? Well, we didn't think we were.

For those of you who were not around or may not remember the very early eighties, let me review what was going on at the time. This was before inexpensive and reliable chemical tests for marijuana, cocaine, and amphetamines were widely available. For the commander of the time, there was essentially no test available for use of common

---

* When problems get out of hand the commanding officer is rightfully often sacrificed first. However, the senior commander must not forget that the problems may be more deep-seated. When you decide that a bad apple must be removed in order to fix a problem—watch that barrel carefully for a while. You may not have gotten all the rot out. Where it is especially bad, you may have done no better than choose at random. You may well have missed the problem.

drugs. Yet he knew there was a drug problem in society. It had been developing for years. Governors, senators, judges, and others had talked openly about their drug use. Some of the states had made the penalty for smoking marijuana no more serious than a jaywalking ticket. Illegal drug use in society was common in the early eighties.

At the same time the submarine force has always considered drug use as essentially incompatible with submarines. Personal responsibility and attention to detail are our key concepts. We are adamantly opposed to people running nuclear reactors, handling nuclear weapons, or operating our submarines when there is any possibility they might be under the influence of drugs.

We were not and are not impressed by people talking about peer pressure, or "social use" of drugs, or excuses about their girlfriends putting marijuana in brownies. We can't use weaklings, either.

The normal penalty for a drug user at that time was pretty uniform around the submarine service. One instance of drug use permanently disqualified the individual from duty in submarines. This, the loss of submarine and nuclear power bonuses, and the average fine and loss of pay grade resulted in a financial penalty for the average person (whose obligated duty requirement did not change) of about $25,000—or a year's salary.

When drug use was detected submariners were encouraged to prosecute the individual and quickly get him off the ship. The premise was that the individual had proven unreliable, so given our public trust with respect to nuclear power and nuclear weapons, we were required to remove his access to both as soon as possible. Given the small size of the submarine, that meant getting him off the ship and up to the squadron.

As the individual was no longer a submariner, his name went to the general surface ship detailer, and the drug abuser was eventually on his way to a surface ship.

When you think about this in retrospect, the situation described did not encourage anyone to get the drug abuser any counselling or assistance. The individual suddenly didn't have anyone who cared about him. The people in the submarine didn't care about him. He had violated their trust. He wasn't even assigned anymore. The squadron didn't care about him—he wasn't going to any of its ships. Any delay in assignment (for example, for drug counselling) was just more time for a foul ball to laze around.

Bottom line—did we put any energy in rehabilitating him? What for? The person had betrayed us. He was never coming back. There was no waiver for someone who was rehabilitated to come back into submarines. He was going far away.

Did the new command rehabilitate him? Nope. Not its problem. He had not been a drug user in that command. He was not someone that command cared about. He was just a new guy.

Think what this looked like to the surface ships that were getting our abusers. This practice had been going on for more than a decade. ("Damn submariners always sending their trash over to us.") More important, think what it looked like to someone interested in the person, such as someone responsible for rehabilitation. We will return to this point.

Now, for a moment, let me explain what the drug problem was doing to the submarines.

You have to appreciate that a submarine is a very small command. There are a hundred-plus people on board who have spent long hours together in demanding situations. There is a lot of informal bonding in a small ship under a large sea.

And each enlisted man aboard has been specially selected from the top cut of all those men coming into the Navy, then sent to school for a year, and then trained on board the submarine for a year or more. Everyone is part of the same team. Everyone on board a submarine has had a part in training each man aboard. Everyone on board has a personal investment in every other man aboard.

A submarine crew is close.

The situation with drugs was one of continuous tension.

Remember that commanders had to act without a reliable test for drugs. They weren't like alcohol. You could smell one beer on someone's breath, and there were easy and reliable breath and blood tests. And drugs weren't something people would ever admit using. Admitting you had been drinking wasn't a violation of law. Someone would just tell you to go sleep it off. Admitting drug use was guaranteeing yourself a $25,000 fine. No one was going to admit drug use.

So we looked for the possession of drug paraphernalia. We were alert for signs of "different lifestyles." We used drug dogs. We did random searches of people, their rooms, and their cars. We used informers. All of us had come into the Navy to be leaders. To keep the world safe for democracy. Instead, we were working our asses off being sons of bitches. And all the while, for fifteen years, surveys reported drug use was increasing in the Navy.

Commanders were trashing some of their best people in order to stop the cancer. They were firing so many people that in some cases we were practically having to reassemble new crews for some submarines. It was a full-court press. And it looked as if we were making progress. In the early eighties we were no longer finding lots of needles, or bags of marijuana, or spaced-out people.

Yet the individuals in charge of counselling and rehabilitating drug abusers reported that we were actually losing. They reported that casual drug use in the Navy was increasing—even approaching fifty percent!*

We people in charge believed the rehabilitators were lying.

Either they were lying, or all the command's efforts were useless. Either the rehabilitators were lying, or all those people whom you had fined and sent to jail had gone in vain. Either they were lying, or the people whom you trusted with your life, who looked you directly in the eye and vowed they didn't—and never would—use drugs were lying. Rehabilitators were often long-haired types themselves. And the music they liked!

Commanders told themselves, and their bosses, and each other, that there might be problems elsewhere in the Navy and the submarine force— but they had licked the drug problem on their ships.

Rehabilitators dealt with drug users every day. Rehabilitators knew we commanders weren't telling the truth. And they were right. The rehabilitators just didn't realize that it wasn't a deliberate lie. We commanders didn't realize we were losing.

The rehabilitators knew that the average sailor used drugs. The rehabilitators knew that the average sailor needed help to overcome peer pressure and get away from drugs. Yet remember that point to which we were going to return. Remember our personnel policies for dealing with drug abusers.

---

* Despite the expense of the testing, which was considerable at the time, the services had done a confidential urinalysis survey in the port that the inspector general was visiting to identify people who had used unauthorized drugs within about the last thirty days. Each year the survey showed an increase in casual drug use. Use was now approaching fifty percent in this port.

From the perspective of the rehabilitators, it was obvious the submarine force was more interested in hammering people than in helping them. Submariners didn't really care about someone who had come in to the rehabilitators for help. Anybody reported as a drug abuser would automatically get thrown out of submarines, and just as automatically lose a third to a half of his salary. The loss of money would make any patient's problem worse, even if his drug use was only a symptom of a deeper problem. And the patient would be transferred immediately. Transferred away from treatment.

So the rehabilitators, in the particular port the inspector general had visited, had decided not to report any drug problems they discovered when treating alcoholics.

That was against the rules.

Funny thing about rules and people. Most people are very uncomfortable not following the established rules—even if they believe the rules are wrong or bad. They have difficulty sleeping at night. Or they gain weight. Something. There are three options for them. First, they can change and follow the rules. That isn't a real option, or they wouldn't be disobeying the rules in the first place. Secondly, they can follow the rules and work to get the rules changed. That's usually too hard. Third, they can disobey the rules and tell someone else. If they do the latter, the responsibility for their disobedience seems magically to be transferred to whomever they have told. I don't understand the mechanism. But people believe it happens. Lucky they do. It's about the only thing that makes law enforcement possible.

Why should the rehabilitators obey the rules and report discovered drug use? They were thinking along the following logic path: The submarine force says there isn't a drug problem on submarines. Any fool knows that drug use really is about twenty to fifty percent. Submariners certainly aren't fools. Therefore submariners must be covering up drug use to avoid throwing people out.

"Well, if we aren't going to report it, I should probably explain why to my girlfriend, the schoolteacher," the rehabilitator said to himself. Who told her sister, the hairdresser. Who told the lady next door. Who told her boyfriend, who happened to work for this guy who he knew was not happy in general with the way the submarine force operated.

And his boss wrote in his diary, "submariners cover up drug use." A couple of months later he gave that diary to the inspector general.

Maybe now you can understand why this one line took us a couple of weeks to unravel. We ended up granting judicial and administrative immunity to get honest testimony. Mixing immunity with lots of late-night interviews, we found out that true drug use aboard submarines was much, much higher than any of us commanders had suspected.

Those damn rehabilitators were right.

What did we learn from this? First of all, the submarine force finally learned how pervasive the drug problem had become, despite the lack of visible evidence (no drugs found on board, no obvious behavior problems, etc.).

No matter how elite the nuclear submarine program, we were not exempt from society's problems. Whether or not they are visible, if warts are growing between the toes of society, you can bet your bottom dollar they are growing somewhere on our submariners. They are also growing on your group, whatever it is.

If you decide your group cannot tolerate some disease society is experiencing, then you have to take real action to eradicate that disease. Real action involves real money. You can't do it on the cheap by improving "leadership."

In submarines we finally decided to pay the price. No matter the cost. We instituted and paid the monetary and personal-privacy price of massive drug testing. Massive, mandatory, observed, and very pervasive drug testing. We forced everyone to become susceptible to a random drug sample four to six times a year. We paid for the drug testing by choosing not to buy a certain number of bullets—or torpedoes. And in a few months drug use in the submarine force plummeted from 40 percent down to less than 1 percent.

Interesting! No education. No counselling. No extra leadership. No nothing. Just the guarantee that if you used drugs you were going to get caught. Now there was good reason to say no to your peers.* If

* Interestingly, we did not find significant drug use among the officers, even with pervasive and monitored drug testing. It wasn't that they weren't monitored. I personally watched a lot of officers provide samples in order to eliminate that possibility. When we started the drug testing we had only one officer positive in the first year (from a group of nearly two thousand). Perhaps the difference was that the officers'

you didn't, you were going to get caught. And you and your peer both knew it.

We commanders (as opposed to the rehabilitators) were right about one thing. Education in this sort of thing is vastly overrated. The only thing that works on a large scale is a system of guaranteed detection and punishment. People turned out to be using drugs not because they had severe personal problems or because the war in Vietnam was causing them such personal anxiety. No. Most people were using drugs because it was "cool." It was cool to be one of the guys and beat the system. When reliable testing made it uncool, drug use stopped faster than a cheap watch.

What else did we learn from this?

First of all, the submarine force had, through years of working hard to screw this up, achieved a reputation for not caring about rehabilitating even the most casual drug user. We also had a reputation for not caring about how we sent our trash to the rest of the Navy to deal with. This reputation made it easy for people to believe the worst about us. People found it easy to believe that submariners were covering up drug abuse—hell, those submariners were probably doing worse than that!

How had we done this? Well, we hadn't thought about the effect of our personnel policies on the rest of the Navy. We had an announced Navy and national policy to rehabilitate drug users who wanted to stop. Yet in submarines we cast people out (and off to the rest of the Navy) without even a casual effort at rehabilitation.

Once we decided that we had a moral obligation to the rest of the Navy to take care of our own problems, as well as an obligation to try to rehabilitate drug abusers, it was easy.

The submarine force had its own surface ships. The people aboard these ships worked as hard as they did aboard other surface ships. And

---

peer group didn't normally use drugs. Even socially. Their peer group was the wardroom—the ten to fifteen other officers that included the commanding officer.

On the other hand, this low officer drug use may indicate that leadership can keep small groups in line against nearly overwhelming pressures. We kept the wardroom (size about ten) pretty much in line and antidrug (I suspect wardroom use at its highest was never more than an experimental ten percent), even when crew (size about a hundred) drug use was approaching fifty percent.

we could make sure the one-time drug abusers were treated fairly—
we had control of the officers commanding these surface ships.

A ready-made solution. We made a rule that people transferred
out of submarines stayed in the submarine force. They went directly
to the facilities and ships that repaired the submarines—in fact, spe-
cifically to the surface ship in the same home port that repaired the
submarine from which the person had just been transferred. Now the
drug offenders were no longer operating our reactors or handling our
nuclear weapons. But they were still in the submarine family.

Immediately, submarine commanding officers started making sure
that they only recommended people for retention in the Navy who looked
susceptible to rehabilitation. And each submarine commanding officer started making sure that every detected drug user went to rehabilitation. Right then. Before the individual left his command. Before
he lost control of him. No one wants a drug user working on his submarine. Since we rehabilitated the ones who could be saved and dis-
charged the rest from the Navy, our surface ships continued to perk
right along.

If one understands the problem, the solution is often obvious.
Difficulties arise when you permit your personal and professional biases
to block you from recognizing all of a problem's facets.

Within a year or two the rest of the Navy started believing we were
treating our people more responsibly. Natural progression of thought.
They were no longer having to clean up our trash. We might even have
actually been doing better.

That was one lesson. It was a lesson combining public relations,
moral integrity, and the best operating policy.

A second lesson was that good leaders have to listen to everyone.
Especially if "everyone" includes types with whom you wouldn't normally
socialize.

If you wear your hair short, be particularly careful that you listen
to those who wear their hair long. If you like and work only with males,
listen to females. If you vote the straight Democratic ticket, listen carefully
when Republicans talk. And vice versa.

Remember: in this little story the rehabilitators were right. Those
pains in the military's side—those liberals—were right. We had a serious
drug problem.

And when you look at lessons, remember that when we finally decided
to spend the money to eliminate drug abuse, it turned out that the tools

(urinalysis testing) already existed. They were expensive, but they existed. Our organization just had to decide to buy them. We didn't have to spend ten or fifteen years in every command wasting every waking hour screwing with the drug problem. We didn't have to lose a decade's worth of all those potentially good people. We could have bought our way out much earlier. We just had to understand the full magnitude of the problem—and understand the limitations of leadership.

The drug issue was the first one in the inspector general's report that caught everyone's attention. It wasn't true that we were deliberately covering up drug abuse aboard submarines. That was absolutely false.

Unfortunately, it was true that failing to pay the price of massive drug testing earlier (it was always available, just expensive) had disguised the extent of the problem. We had not evaluated exactly why the submarine force was different from the rest of the Navy, taken the next step, and instituted drug testing. We had gone along with the rest of the Navy and the nation in using half-measures to address a problem that for us was integral to the very core of the nuclear submarine program. We had failed to recognize that our young people inevitably reflected society.

We relied on leadership for years. Leadership didn't fix the problem. Money fixed it.

So why do we end up with situations in which leadership is not enough? How do we recognize them? What do we do?

The first part is simple. We can overwhelm anyone or any group. We can always give a group a task too difficult. Which means that we will always have situations that need more than leadership. The real problem is to discover how we recognize and fix the situation without letting it mildew until it stinks.

The key is to be alert to failure. We often are too cavalier when a command is having problems. We expect everyone to have mishaps sometime, and often the immediate supervisors want to maintain their distance so they don't become "part of the problem." But a problem is a bump in the road that was caused by something.

If it is not a problem of an individual in the command and is not caused by a command policy, then is it a policy problem from further up the line? There is always a reason. You may not be able to figure it out, but there is always a reason. File unexplained bumps away, worry them in your spare moments like a cow worries its cud. And keep the file open.

Also be attentive to situations in which you are not spending a lot of resources to solve the problem. Your most limited resources are always good people and lots of money. When you are not applying those key resources to solve a problem, then make sure this is a deliberate choice. Leadership and hard work have their limits. Make sure you can afford a cheap solution.

# CHAPTER ELEVEN

## One-Two

One of the best leaders I ever worked for taught me the old one-two.

In boxing, "the old one-two" is verbal shorthand for the setup jab followed by the knockout punch. In leadership, "the old one-two" refers to how a supervisor focuses people's attentions and energies.

There are two aspects to this focusing. The first has to do with the key things you want people to remember. Think of how many times you have heard someone say, "I want you to remember the following fourteen items. . . ."

Not very many times? Probably none, unless you have worked for someone dumb. People don't remember fourteen things well. They don't remember eighteen. They don't even reliably remember the six additional ways someone can score from third base (as compared to being on second). How can you expect them to remember something less important?

People remember things on the order of three or fewer. I don't know why. However, just like Aladdin's genie's wishes, a leader is limited to no more than three. When you want to establish rules you want remembered *every time,* then you have to reduce your expectations so they can be covered in your own three wishes.

That limitation isn't as confining as one might initially think. It is surprising what complex issues can be reduced to a few essential rules. For example, the operation of a submarine's nuclear reactor requires bright people and years of training. Yet everything involved in the design, construction, and operation of a pressurized water reactor is derived from one simple rule: "Keep the core covered (with water)." You don't need any other rule. If you design, build, and operate the reactor with that one rule in mind, you will do so correctly. Therefore, in submarines we drive that one rule into everyone's subconscious. If an individual can't remember that rule, he can't stay around.

Try this exercise to test your leadership magic. Think about what your group is going to be doing for the next substantial chunk of time. Don't worry about periods shorter than a few months. Remember that you are going to try to find some golden rules you want to follow. Trying to train everyone for some special event only a week or two long is usually wasted effort.

Now, what are the results you expect? Better still, what are the optimum results and what are the minimum results you will accept? You are probably going to have more than three at the start, so I recommend you write them down. Then, looking at what you have written, what are the one or two key things your people must accomplish to get where you want to go?

This last evaluation isn't simple. It often requires significant imagination and visualization on your part. But I have always found that when I have reduced the rules down to the very few I want my people always to follow, I magically find that I also understand better what must happen in order for my organization to be successful.

Let me give you an example. One time we were going to take a submarine into an overhaul period. What were the rules we wanted everyone to follow?

The inexperienced commanding officer may well dwell on the fact that his boss is paying for this overhaul. Therefore, given how expensive it is each day the ship is in the yard, the commanding officer might logically write down as one of his three goals that he wants to get out of the overhaul early. Sounds good. Schedules are important or they wouldn't be made. Being on time might even look good to his boss. Piety is always praised.

However, establishing such a goal for the crew would not be very useful. The work package on the submarine averages about 200,000 man-days and a hundred million dollars. To accomplish this work, a large submarine shipyard has ten to fifteen thousand workers, and subcontracts a great deal of the work involved in a submarine overhaul to other companies that also have thousands of workers. A submarine in overhaul has a crew of about 140. What impact do you think the submarine's crew's efforts have on the pace of the overhaul?

Right, the five-hundred-pound canary in the overhaul cage is not the ship's crew. The crew can screw up the schedule by not being ready for specific events, but they can't make the perch swing unless the shipyard canary shifts its weight.

So, what does the leader in an overhaul want?

On this occasion, as our ship was on its way to overhaul we thought about this and decided that it was our own responsibility as leaders to try to motivate the shipyard canary. Therefore we wouldn't talk to the crew about completing overhaul on time. What we actually wanted our people to do could be boiled down to two things. First, we wanted the crew to operate correctly and safely. Second, we wanted everyone to be prepared to support the shipyard whenever they wanted to do work (never give the shipyard canary an excuse to eat aboard another ship). Our optimum results were that we would complete overhaul early. But our minimum acceptable results didn't involve time at all. Our acceptable results were that all the equipment would work properly when we finished overhaul and that no one would have gotten hurt in the process.

Our acceptable results were still too general. What the crew needed was something more tangible.

We thought again. The essence of the safety program aboard a ship is what is called the tag-out system. Everything that is dangerous receives a red tag, and you can't operate it without getting special permission and physically taking the tag off. Something that requires special thought but isn't inherently dangerous receives a yellow tag.

There is a great deal involved in making all the decisions as to which items require tags, which do not, and how the system is controlled. A typical overhaul involves the placement or removal of hundreds of thousands of red or yellow tags—with a system of multiple signatures behind each tag recording exactly who approved and/or did exactly what. If the system operates completely correctly, equipment isn't damaged and people aren't hurt.

So we established, as rule one, that we wanted everyone to use the tag-out system properly. And to ensure that everyone knew we were serious, we added that the improper use of the tag-out system would result in a hundred-dollar fine. Per tag. For everyone involved.

It happened only once.

With literally hundreds of thousands of opportunities for human beings to make an error, how could we expect perfect performance? Two reasons. First, we didn't establish a rule we didn't really care about—no basic rules about areas where we could tolerate occasional errors. Second, people can do error-free work—as long as they care to. Admiral Rickover used to note that in their lifetimes people go home tens of thousands of times. The average worker never goes home to the wrong house.

With this one rule we solved many problems. Almost everybody is motivated to do well. Problems occur when people are too tired to do good work, or don't understand what they are doing, or aren't properly trained to do what they should. The tag-out system is integral to all work in the shipyard. But motivated people are reluctant to admit they don't know how to do something or are just too tired to think. Their "can-do" spirit can inadvertently bypass a hundred such systems. A hundred dollars a tag was enough to overcome those inhibitions. Because the fine also applied to all the supervisors, the supervisors had a great deal of incentive to ensure they were actually supervising—that unqualified people didn't get assigned or permitted to do improper work.

In a two-year overhaul, we didn't have problems with people doing work when they were too tired. We didn't have problems with people authorizing improper work. We didn't have problems with people doing work who weren't qualified. No one was hurt. No equipment was damaged.

And people had to remember only one rule.

A leader who fully understands what he wants the organization to achieve, as well as what he expects from his people (and the two are often not the same), can reduce his desires to a very few rules. So long as that number is no more than the chances Aladdin had, you will have the opportunity to achieve truly magical results, as he did.

I said that there were two aspects to focussing the efforts of your people. The first had to do with making magical wishes. The second has to do with equally impressive goal-setting.

The exceptional leader can identify desirable organizational goals that are not obvious to the average person. It's more than insight. Some people operate on another plane of consciousness. If you give everybody the same set of facts, the same observables, and ask where the organization should proceed, most people are going to point in one general direction. There are some leaders, however, who somehow sense that the best goal is not down in the hollow by the stream, but lies unseen over the hill.

When we followers get over the hill, and see the lake and the acres of arable land, we are always dazzled by his perception.*

I can't explain how some people sense what's over the hill. It has to involve something with the gods. So I don't worry about it. What is at least as interesting for us mortals is that the exceptional leader is able to get a thirsty organization to take the hard path over the hill instead of following the valley down to the visible, sparkling stream. He is able to do so because of the old "one or two."

Any leader can demand and get from his people one or two extraordinary achievements. I am not talking about the progress you get through everyone's steady, excellent work, or the performance you can get by training, improving the standards, asking for more, and making your people better workers. Both those processes often produce remarkable results in the long run. However, what I am referring to is when the leader says, "I want that," and the organization collectively turns around and looks at itself.

In the beginning, it is impossible to get "that." No one knows how to start. No one knows where the hell it even is. No one knows how to get there. It's probably against the rules to have "that." Besides, no one in the organization has absolutely any idea what he would do with "that" if he had it.

Doesn't matter. In nearly all cases, a leader can demand that an organization give him one or two "thats." The leader has to be wise. Whether he appears to be doing so or not, he has to always watch the organization to ensure it doesn't destroy itself getting "that." He has to stop efforts that waste assets on pursuits down obviously wrong roads.

---

* A good example of this occurred when Admiral Zumwalt relieved his predecessor as the chief of naval operations in 1970. At that time, the Navy and the rest of the Department of Defense, as well as the country, were focussed on the war in Vietnam. Admiral Zumwalt soon gave the task of supporting the war to a junior subordinate to handle. Admiral Zumwalt was convinced that the nation's and the Navy's best interests were not tied up with success in the war in Vietnam, but rather were dependent on the military being able to attract and recruit sufficient qualified people, many of whom would have to be minorities, to serve in the coming decades. Therefore, he chose to work personally on improving the Navy's treatment of, and image with, minorities.

But if he keeps the pressure on, if he does not let the organization forget about the one thing he wants, he can get it.

There are lots of interesting bureaucratic methods of getting what you want. One of the easiest is to chair a meeting once a week or once a month that addresses only the status of achieving "that." Never let the meeting be skipped. Give each supervisor personal responsibility for some aspect. Never let anyone be excused from the meeting. Make each supervisor talk about what he has done to get "that." Keep minutes. Publish them. Reward someone for partially achieving what you wanted. Publicly promise you will get "that." Have your senior staff stand beside you when you promise. You can get it.

And if you limit yourself to one or two of those special "thats," you can get them without significantly disrupting the organization's accomplishment of whatever else it is normally supposed to be doing.

It's the old one or two.

Getting "thats" is the easy part.

Now all you have to do is convince the gods to help you think of them.

# CHAPTER TWELVE

## Up Or

P eople are every organization's most important asset. This is a fact, not a theory. A good organization spends a great deal of effort attracting and recruiting the right people, sorting the good from the bad, and ensuring it keeps the good ones. Conventional wisdom's most hoary fact is that people are important. It is thus not surprising that many companies enunciate a propeople policy. However, it is amazing how many organizations forget this principle when times get a little tough. This is a story about one organization that forgot.

The story starts during the last couple of years of the Vietnam War. For those who weren't around, by the early seventies even the military knew that we weren't winning, and everybody knew Vietnam was not a popular war. The last sentence understates the facts. After the excitement of the first resolutions wore away, I don't think it ever was a popular war.

It was also not a popular war in the Navy. The Navy leadership was concerned that after the war was over, there would not be enough Navy left to maintain the necessary United States presence around the globe. It wasn't a problem with the Viet Cong sinking ships, it was a concern that the ships might very well rust away. The average age of Navy ships skyrocketed during the war.

In retrospect it is easy to see how it happened. It was even fairly evident at the time. A continuously growing number of congressmen wanted to make every Defense Department appropriation a new battleground to challenge the administration about the war. Even those congressmen who supported the war effort were interested in keeping total defense costs as low as possible to avoid the national firestorm that a tax increase would bring. Thus, year after year, the Navy ate down its weapons stocks and, after that particular cupboard was bare, took money originally earmarked for buying new ships and airplanes and instead bought shells and bombs. As a direct result, each year the fleet got another year older. Like innumerable other companies that have fallen by the wayside over the decades, the Navy was simply not making an adequate investment in capital improvements.

The Navy did not lack for people pointing out the signs of decay and drawing comparisons to postwar England and the Roman Empire. By the early seventies every analyst worth his salt had several graphs in his or her briefcase showing the age of the ships in the fleet broken down by class, tonnage, caliber of gun, and anything else the analyst could conceive. And the analyst could also show how budget investments were split by percentages—so much for shipbuilding, so much for expenses to operate bases, so much for fuel, so much for bombs and bullets, so much for people, and so on. Everyone is always interested in pictures, predictions, and how the trend lines lie.

It was clear that the rate of shipbuilding had for some time been heading south.

It also was readily apparent that sailors' salaries were consuming a higher and higher percentage of our discretionary dollars. It wasn't that we were paying princely wages to our sailors, it was that during wartime the dollars spent on bombs aren't discretionary. The metal you intend to send the other guy's way is not an optional purchase. We therefore didn't have much money left for ships.

As a result, when the inevitable pie of different-colored money shares appeared on analysts' charts, the slice labeled "personnel costs" seemed to grow larger with every reiteration. Sometimes that particular slice was even colored a vivid purple, so that *the problem* hammered itself into everyone's consciousness.

I cannot speak for other times and other places, but I do know that in 1973 around Washington and the Navy a great number of people, including the Navy's senior leadership, were focussed on the increasing cost of sailors' salaries. The Navy couldn't do much about extracting itself from the war—that was up to the president, the Congress, and Hanoi. The Navy couldn't do anything about extra money to buy ships—that was tied up in the same circuit. But there are people in the Pentagon assigned to worry about where each dollar is going, and they are going to worry. It was impolitic to talk about the increasing cost of the war, so Navy leadership talked about the increasing cost of people.

In response, every analyst around town produced charts and viewgraphs as to how much "people" costs had risen proportionally over the past ten years, and what extraordinary heights those expenses might reach over the next ten.*

A lot of trees died in order to record these concerns adequately.

Skip ahead two or three years. The war is finally over. At corporate headquarters in Washington the Navy is trying to rebuild the fleet and replenish its weapons stocks. In the meantime, what is happening out in the fleet?

The sailors are working their butts off to bring the new ships (for which there is now sufficient money) on-line, to keep the older ships working until they can be replaced, to survive the ugly postwar public attitude toward anything military, and to sail at a pace sufficient to keep the rest of the world respectful toward United States interests—which is not a small task immediately after losing a very public war to a very, very Third-World power. The sailors were busy.

The leaders in Washington were still worried about the cost of people.

To understand the next point, you must have a little perspective. Congressmen do not normally line up to ladle out taxpayer money for military salaries. Sailors tend to be concentrated in a few states, relatively rootless, restricted from personally participating in partisan politics, and small fry in the political fund-raising world. On the other hand, Congressional appropriations that go to buy trucks and tanks and airplanes and ships can be directed to any region, state, or district in the Union and go directly to taxpayers—through entities that are large employers in a community, large local presences, and perhaps even large political contributors.

---

* I remember worrying about how soon people costs were going to be more than fifty percent of every dollar the Navy spent. At the time, everyone was talking about that certainty and what awful things that portended for the Navy. Nearly twenty years later I recomputed all the data and found, to my surprise, that personnel costs had never risen above thirty-five percent. In retrospect, what we had been fearing should not have worried anyone. As soon as we weren't fighting a war and there was money to buy ships the relative cost of sailors dropped again. It seems obvious now. It wasn't at the time.

Sailors get raises only when the Army, Navy, and Air Force keep a constant man-to-man press on the Congress. In the years following the end of the Vietnam War sailors' salaries fell significantly relative to inflation and equivalent civilian salaries.*

Why? Perhaps because the Defense Department leadership wasn't working to increase or even maintain the worker's benefits package. Perhaps our leadership was frozen in place by all the analysts' charts showing the rising "people costs." Let me relate a story that reflects this attitude.

While the average citizen may well not realize this, when we recruit sailors we often sign them to contracts with significantly different incentives, depending on the potential of the person and the recruiting environment. As a specific and pertinent example, if a man or woman looks bright and motivated enough to learn to repair computers and highly complex electronic equipment, he or she is going to be offered a better contract than someone not so capable. The Navy is not exempt from the marketplace laws of supply and demand.

In the time frame of interest, the Navy was offering contracts called "four by twos" to the best enlisted people we could recruit. The top few percent of the recruits signed up for a year or more of specialized schooling in electronics, computers, or nuclear engineering. The sailor so selected then went to a ship for practical instruction and application. He was inevitably not very valuable to the ship upon arrival, and it required a year or two of on-the-job training before the sailor started to pay back the Navy's investment. But because the individual had received the schoolroom and practical training he was exceptionally employable in the civilian marketplace. That presented the Navy with a dilemma.

Four years service was the longest contract the rules allowed the Navy to write for initial recruits. But the Navy wanted more than two to three years payback in exchange for the expensive schooling and practical training it was providing each of these special sailors. So we wrote "four by two" contracts that obligated the sailor for four years and then, in effect, gave the Navy the right to exercise a two-year extension to that contract at the end of those four years. However (please try to

---

* By about 40 percent over a period of five years.

follow this, it will be important to understanding the issue), the individual could elect, up to the day the Navy exercised the extension to that contract, to sign a new contract for three years or more, *which automatically canceled the extension* and paid the sailor a signing bonus of about fifteen to twenty thousand dollars (almost equivalent to a year's salary for the sailor). Alternatively, if the sailor permitted the extension to go into effect, he not only owed the government two more years service but was giving up the equivalent of double pay for the third year. As a practical matter, nearly every sailor recruited in this category, whatever his personal plans with respect to a career in the Navy, opted to cancel his two-year extension in exchange for another obligated year at double salary.

And then one day a Navy notice went out to each ship that talked about how hard times were and the need to save some money. The notice then announced that henceforth no one would be permitted to cancel his extension by reenlisting. This new policy affected only the "four by twos." Effectively, each of the "special sailors," these particularly bright and motivated people we had recruited, was told that he was personally going to contribute fifteen to twenty thousand dollars to solve a Navy funding problem. As the special sailors were a relatively small group, the savings were about the same as the cost of one or two missiles, or a tenth of an airplane, or one one-hundredth of the cost of a ship.

The special sailors were all bright people. And each sailor quickly remembered that he and a Navy representative had signed a contract specifying both the Navy's and the sailor's rights (and the sailor's right to cancel the extension as I have discussed above and receive a bonus was clear). The sailors brought their complaint to their supervisors.

What happened next has embarrassed me for twenty years.

Anyone can make an error, and a fool at a clerk level can often make the organization look stupid initially. But there is no excuse when an error is brought to a senior manager's attention and still nothing is done to correct the problem.

In this particular case, four different organizational levels of our company did nothing to fix the problem, and did not even support the principle of fair play. The only ship that championed the sailors' cause was finally told, in writing, that not only was there no problem, the fact that the ship had raised the problem demonstrated a lack of senior leadership aboard that unit.

Some sailors in another port decided to take matters into their own hands. They hired a civilian lawyer who filed a class-action suit. The suit was settled in about a year, when the judge found for each and every one of the sailors and directed that the Navy pay treble damages. Of course, by that time all the sailors who had been wronged had gotten out of the Navy, as had their friends—for who would stay with an organization that had violated the only contract a sailor had? Besides, if you were one of those sailors' peers, you also had to leave the Navy. If you stayed you were siding with the Navy against your friend. And we in the Navy leadership were clearly in the wrong.*

The Navy lost a lot of good people.

How in the world did we get in that situation? It was only when I eventually became relatively senior and was worrying myself about how much personnel costs were going up that I realized what had happened. Our middle management had become so concerned about rising personnel costs that they had lost the ability to evaluate people issues objectively. They had lost perspective. They had forgotten that people were their most important asset. The costs of this memory hiccup had been considerable. They would grow even higher.

Skip ahead another five years.

I was aboard a submarine. A submarine is a very potent force, powered by a nuclear reactor and possibly armed with nuclear weapons. Given the difficulty and criticality of the submarine mission along with the small size of the crew, submarines have historically received a disproportionate share of the cream of the sailors recruited into the Navy. In any twelve months, probably the worst sailor admitted into submarines would rank no lower than the top ten percent of all the sailors recruited that year.

---

* Which does not mean that the secretary of the Navy or the chief of naval operations ever knew of this problem. Unfortunately, while juniors believe that seniors know about everything that is going on, that is completely false. Senior leadership is worried about issues that you don't even know exist. They assume things are going well. Seniors seldom know about dumb things. They didn't get where they are by being stupid. Tell them. Tell them officially and personally. Ensure they understand. It is the only way that the organization has a fair chance to correct wrongs.

About thirty to forty men rotate into the ship's crew each year, and each crew tends to get new people aboard in twos and threes. I will always remember the day we came into port after a short underway period and found two new replacements waiting on the pier. Good. We were four men short and were on our way to a six-month deployment overseas. Unfortunately, there was a minor problem. When we reviewed their records we found that both were convicted murderers!

One had stabbed someone over a girl. The second had put a .45 slug in the chest of the person who sat behind him in high school. You could understand why. His story was that the son of a bitch always chewed gum with his mouth open. He had also had an unfortunate incident in boot camp. His rifle had gone off accidentally and injured his drill instructor. We left both men on the pier when we sailed.

That was the low point for the Navy by my personal measurement. By the time we returned to the States after deployment, the Reagan revolution was well underway and the country was again investing money in the military. Because money was available there was also money for people, and some wise leaders paid a great deal of attention to taking better care of people. The 1991 Desert Storm results were the proof of that particular pudding.

People are any organization's most important asset. When you are a manager you realize that what you can accomplish is limited only by the small number of take-charge people you can personally tap and press into service. There are more problems than leaders. A competent person who has been trained and inculcated is not a trivial organizational asset. An extraordinary individual who can truly lead is nearly invaluable.

At the same time, if your personnel policies start to turn people off, remember that, despite conventional wisdom, you never lose the deadwood first.* At first blush it seems you will, because your good people are motivated, involved, and interested in your organization, while the deadwood had been thinking about leaving anyway.

---

* Which doesn't mean that you should let the deadwood remain. It does mean that you must use some method to root it out, and you must be even more ruthless in difficult times. Getting rid of the least productive members leaves more assets to keep the better people.

I will tell you from experience that the facts are exactly opposite. Your good people are easily employable somewhere else. On the other hand, very few other people will be dumb enough to offer your dead-wood a job. If you don't deliberately take care of all your people, in down cycles as well as good times, your good people will find a reason to drift away. One day you will turn around and realize you are trying to run the organization with a collection of deadwood and driftwood. You have your old deadwood and some new driftwood you were forced to hire because you weren't able to attract good people anymore.

There are problems that leadership can't solve. One of these can be an organization's unwillingness to spend the time and money to attract, recruit, sort, and keep good people. On the other hand, good leadership keeps the organization focussed on the importance of quality people. Good leadership doesn't permit cyclic tough times and the accompanying transitory panic to distract the group from the most important issue. And the most important issue always remains good people, in either up or down cycles.

# CHAPTER THIRTEEN

## Egregious

I t's one of those words that telegraphs its meaning. Roll it off your tongue—it even sounds bad. Lawyers use this word a lot. During class in law school, they write it on notes and pass them around the room. Wherever attorneys congregate, they scrawl *egregious* in the restroom stalls.

Egregious means "especially bad, flagrant"—no one could be that bad without deliberately trying.

In my experience it isn't usually true. People don't deliberately try to do badly. The results may truly be terrible. But the actions weren't deliberate.

Well, if they are not deliberate, then how do such gross things happen? Good question. Perhaps a story. . . .

Several years ago I was involved in the investigation of three unrelated incidents. Each was different. Each was serious. Although the incidents appeared unconnected, after a while it became apparent there was one common denominator.

Remember that in the chapter "Limits" there was a problem besides drug abuse in the inspector general's report that had caught everyone's eye. That problem revolved around three submarine commanding officers who were accused of alcoholism.

We needed to get to the truth quickly. We did. The investigation was much more direct and easier than the drug investigation had been. One of the accused commanding officers was a documented teetotaler. Another was almost equally a goody-goody—he had even reported another commanding officer for drinking too much. The third officer was evaluated as one of the very top commanders of the eight exceptional ones in his squadron (two later made admiral, five were promoted to captain).

Before we talk about this last commanding officer, whom everyone admitted drank a bit, you need a little historical background.

Submariners remember several facts from World War II. One is that a higher percentage of submariners gave their lives than did the men in any other group in the war. There were several simple reasons for this fact. To begin with, when a submarine went down it generally took the entire crew. Secondly, United States submarines were on the front line for the entire war. They operated without air control or other help. Remember that one of the first three submarines under way after Pearl Harbor sailed right into Tokyo Bay, where she attacked a ship and first carried the war home to the Japanese.

A lot of submarines went down during World War II. A lot of submariners died.

The second thing submariners remember from World War II is that a lot of these men died because their weapons didn't work. It was a scandal. You can read the details in history books. The torpedoes simply didn't explode, no matter how carefully and exactly they were placed. Today we go to a great deal of effort to ensure our weapons are realistically tested during peacetime—so they will work during wartime.

The third key thing submariners remember from World War II is that between the World Wars we had effectively selected the warriors out of command. We had inadvertently emphasized risk avoidance instead of risk evaluation. We had emphasized survival rather than success. We had graded people by the results of in-port inspections rather than by performance at sea. When the Second World War started our commanding officers were not very effective. Essentially, the admirals had to order in a second generation of submarine commanding officers before the submarines started to rack up the impressive kill list that is the best-remembered submarine legacy from World War II.

The world has changed since World War II. For one thing, the nuclear submarine has been invented and has taken its place as the preeminent naval vessel. However, the three key lessons of that last world conflict are still applicable. And, if we have a world war during the next several decades, the nuclear submarine will be the capital ship of that war. Therefore, it is even more important that we do not make the same type of mistakes we made during the peace before the last great war.

To this day, senior submarine officers live with some very specific charges handed down from their World War II predecessors: ensure we breed aggressive warriors who are willing to die for their country; ensure their day-to-day training is so realistic that all equipment is always ready; ensure we do not again select out the tigers and leave ourselves with only the lambs.

So we have been relatively lenient in how we treat those young officers who may move in what others might consider overly broad swaths. In how we treat those who seem to do those things that indicate a relatively high level of testosterone. Those who may drink a bit. Who may pursue the girls a little.

We want warriors. If they run an aggressive ship, if they are operationally successful—we keep them, and keep them in command. We would rather have a tiger of any breed than the purest Merino sheep.

End of historic background.

One of the commanding officers the inspector general had reported to be an alcoholic turned out to be the same commanding officer whom one of his peers had reported as an excessive drinker. But he was one of our most aggressive commanders.

He was not your average guy in many ways. He had a gorgeous mistress. Absolutely gorgeous. Kept her for years. And his wife didn't seem to mind. There were lots of stories about ports his ship had pulled into where the mistress had been on the pier instead of his wife. They were both good-looking and intelligent women. I admired them both.

People had worried about his drinking before. A year earlier his commander had sent him for a special medical evaluation by an alcoholism specialist. The handwritten evaluation, dutifully placed in his record, started out, "Commander Smith does not display any of the clinical hard signs of alcoholism" and then trailed off into the general unreadable scrawl that some doctors seem to mistake as a sign of good breeding or high intelligence.

We dutifully commenced the investigation. Some smoke. No flames. True, he was not the typical husband. But, as I have noted, we aren't necessarily interested in someone who fits nicely into a neighborhood of picket fences and soap salesmen. We are interested in leaders. Men who can operate nuclear submarines with flair, dash, and success.

We talked to men on his crew. They loved him. He was thoughtful about them. He was interested in them. They uniformly trusted his judgment (which was particularly impressive, because one of his officers had run the submarine into the ocean bottom a couple of months earlier, and there had been some question whether the commanding officer had done all he should have). Interesting—a leader who was effective and whom his people truly liked. A rare find. No wonder he was ranked so highly among his peers.

We interviewed the people he had recently worked for. Several different supervisors were called. They had gone to dinner with the man. And his wife. Things had gone well. The man didn't even drink much. Maybe a glass of wine before dinner. Maybe another with. No evidence at all of excess. Looks like he's even getting back together with his wife.

And then we started calling men across the country who had previously served with the commanding officer and had then gotten out of the Navy and gone back to work at various occupations in civilian life. This was not my idea. I was ready to quit this part of the investigation. We had already talked to dozens of people. We had the medical officer's statement. His bosses' statements. His people's statements. What the hell?

The admiral in charge of the investigation insisted that we do something more. His instinct was that something was wrong. So we called people who used to be on the submarine.

They all said the same thing. We would start by identifying ourselves and telling them that we had some unsubstantiated allegations about excessive use of alcohol on their old submarine, and we were just following up. . . .

And each of them said something like, "By golly, it has taken you guys long enough. That man is a drunk. He drank every day in port. He drank in the morning. His breath would knock over a skunk. Hell, he couldn't even hold a pen to do paperwork because his hands shook so much. I got out of the Navy because I knew you people knew he was a drunk and didn't care about us. . . ."

Son of a bitch!

So we took the medical evaluation back down to the doctor who had written it and sat him down and put him under oath and asked him to read what he had written on his evaluation. And that wimp put on his glasses and looked at the unreadable record he had made and said, "Of course, gentlemen, I wrote, 'Commander Smith does not have any of the hard signs of alcoholism . . . but he is well known to all of us in the profession as the most egregious alcoholic in this city and in the submarine force. He drinks more than a fifth of Scotch a day, is never not under the influence of alcohol, and it is only a matter of time before he suffers irreversible liver damage. His situation is not assisted by his wife, who is probably also an alcoholic. . . .''

And about then, one of the man's bosses called us up long distance and said, "You know, you asked about Commander Smith's drinking, and I told you I didn't see anything in the week he stayed with me, but my wife tells me the trash man commented to one of our neighbors, and she, our neighbor, told my wife that he, the trash man, was surprised that we had one trash can completely full of Scotch bottles last week. He goes by the front of the house every day and hadn't even noticed us preparing for a party."

It went downhill from there. Ended up with the commanding officer getting relieved (not before he again ran his ship aground), and being sent to alcohol rehabilitation.

I learned one thing. Everyone who works for an alcoholic protects him. Doesn't make any sense. The alcoholic is putting everyone on his ship in danger. But people protect him. Something in raw human nature. They'll lie for him and cover for him. Against the organization. Against their own best interests.

I also learned how hard it is to identify an alcoholic and how long an alcoholic survives in an organization. His bosses and peers seldom see any signs. Perhaps we are all so involved in our own worries that we don't look hard enough. But if the bosses and peers don't see it, and the subordinates are covering it up—makes it awfully hard to identify the situation. The typical alcoholic goes undetected for a long time.

If you are in a profession that can't afford alcoholics in responsible positions, don't count on medical or other special groups to help you identify the secret alcoholic. Those "helpers" are not leadership people. If they were, they wouldn't be in those professions. They are not going to help you make hard decisions that are directly going to affect an alcoholic's ability to make a living. They are trying to help the individual.

You are also trying to help the individual, but with you the group necessarily is going to come first. You are interested in keeping the organization healthy—if required, at the expense of the individual. The outfit may be willing to take a rehabilitated alcoholic back, but in most institutions, in all candor, there is always some cost to the individual. He may lose seniority, or there may be jobs for which he is no longer suited. Something.

The medical or rehabilitation groups are not going to help you identify someone to cut out of your organization. Too tough for them. You are on your own. If it is also usually too tough for you, you are in the majority.

Doesn't mean you are a good leader—but you *are* in the majority.

The second investigation was even more serious than the first. Several men aboard one of our submarines had been killed. Some of us were assigned to find out how and why.

The how was easy.

The submarine that had the accident was a submarine that was specially configured to operate with underwater divers. Being able to release underwater swimmers surreptitiously at different places in the world and later—equally surreptitiously—recover those same swimmers has some interesting uses in a hostile world.

At the same time, the United States Navy has men especially trained as underwater swimmers, called SEALs, and a submarine is a particularly fine surreptitious platform.

To maintain any military capability requires practice. In this case the SEALs need to practice aboard the submarine at sea. The submarine with the SEALs aboard had left port the morning of the incident and gone to sea for the day. After a few hours the submarine arrived at the desired location and slowly stopped and carefully balanced itself in the water. The SEALs, each breathing by means of individual scuba gear, left the submarine proper and entered a large special chamber welded to the top of the submarine. Once inside, they flooded the chamber with water to equalize the pressure inside the chamber with the pressure of the seawater outside. Then the SEALs opened the chamber door and left the submarine for an underwater swimming exercise.

Returning to the submarine was achieved by reversing the process. The men entered the chamber and closed the door. Then they drained the water while admitting air to equalize the chamber's pressure with the submarine's atmosphere.

The problem occurred immediately after the SEALs returned to the chamber and closed the door. They had next opened a large valve to drain the chamber so they could return to the submarine. The water immediately began to rush out the huge drain valve with its normal loud roar. The level in the chamber dropped below the level of the men's shoulders. You would think any danger was past.

Not true. Unfortunately, someone had failed to open the valve that let in the compensating air. There was nothing to fill the empty volume left by the receding water. It was as if a window—a picture window—

had suddenly blown out of an airliner at fifty thousand feet. Instant vacuum. But there wasn't any noise more than the normal sound of the water rushing out. The men inside the chamber instantly lost consciousness. No one outside the chamber knew anything wrong had occurred. By the time the ship's crew opened the chamber door five of the six men inside were dead.

Terribly sad, emotional time. One death is always a shock in a small organization. Multiple deaths are nearly unbearable.

We had a hearing and looked at personal and organizational responsibility. We determined how we could prevent a vacuum from unexpectedly developing again. We looked at each submarine (all use a similar chamber for emergency underwater egress from the submarine), to make sure we didn't have similar problems elsewhere. The whole submarine force worked at fixing the problem with our usual efficiency and thoroughness.

After a few weeks the investigation had been finished. Corrective action taken. Reports filed. The guilty hung. The whole thing tidied up and handed over to the lawyers to appeal and argue about for the rest of the decade.

One problem.

We knew how it happened. One guy didn't open the vent valve to let the air in.

We didn't know why.

The team operating the valves were men assigned to the submarine. They were inside the chamber with two SEALs. There was one second class petty officer, one chief, and two seamen. The chief was the only one who survived.

Although he was senior, the chief was actually not in charge. He had recently reported to the ship and was in the process of being trained. The second class petty officer was the person responsible for operating the chamber from what was descriptively called the "wet" side.

The second class petty officer was an interesting individual. His record was absolutely impeccable. He had been considered to be the most knowledgeable person in the crew on the entire diving system. He was in excellent physical shape. He had advanced in rate as fast as possible, indicating that he was both intelligent and mature. He was the only second class petty officer on the submarine qualified to be in charge.

After the incident there was a great deal of recrimination and finger-pointing by individuals in the crew. That's natural. No one wants to think that his error killed someone. And we found a lot of things we didn't like about the way that particular ship was run. But everyone, officer and enlisted, aboard that submarine was unanimous in one respect. They each thought the second class was one of the most outstanding men aboard.

That bothered the investigators. Usually your best people are not involved and definitely are not the cause of a problem. Usually your problems come when, and precisely because, your best people are not involved. Good people, even in bad organizations, always seem to find some way of side-stepping trouble.

Why had the submarine's best man caused a casualty that killed five men?

And why was the chief the only one who lived?

Well, no one knew for sure. The best guess was that the chief had lived because he had stayed conscious for one-half second longer than anyone else, and had managed to hook his arm over a pipe. When he lost consciousness in the vacuum his arm had caught between the pipe and a cable and held his face clear of the residual water in the chamber. The rest of the men had fallen into the water when they had passed out.

We had no idea why the chief had stayed conscious for a little longer. When he testified he couldn't remember anything of what had happened—just remembered hooking his arm over a pipe and lots of blackness. Looked like he was a victim of stress memory blocking. Maybe the chief had stayed conscious a little longer because he was in better shape?

No. We had seen him smoking. He was at least ten years older than the others. And we later found he had a history of drinking excessively.

Maybe he was held up by the second class? The second class had been a marathon runner. Logically, he should have maintained consciousness a little longer than the others. Yet his body was found underneath where the chief had been standing, his hands near the valve that should have been opened all the way, and was found only partially so.

Well, the investigators had determined what had actually caused the deaths. We had found what we had to change. And all the people who had been in the chamber were dead or didn't remember anything. Not a lot to be gained by continuing to worry about some details that didn't matter. We had already decided to replace the submarine's leadership structure. Why saddle the only living guy with some guilt that he might not deserve?

So we decided that the dead second class had inexplicably failed to open the proper valve all the way and let it go.

But in our hearts we knew there was a loose end dangling somewhere.

Several months later a couple more clues crossed our desks. First of all, the new leadership in the command ordered the chief into a hospital for mandatory alcohol rehabilitation. Then the chief got in trouble with drugs and wrote a letter to a friend, talking about all the things that had happened to him in the last few months and asking for help.

The letter was interesting. His friend passed it on to us.

The chief wrote that he had been an alcoholic for a long time.

The chief wrote that he had been drinking heavily the night before the submarine's tragic underway. The same way he did every night. And the chief told his friend that the casualty had all been his fault—and he had used drugs later only "to forget." He didn't share any details about how the accident was his fault. He didn't want to comment later when we asked him about the letter.

So we thought about the problem again. If the chief was the trainee in the chamber, then it was logical that the chief was probably the one operating the valves under the supervision of the second class. If the chief had still been under the influence of alcohol, then he might have mistakenly opened the valve only partially.

The second class had been really sharp. When he sensed the loss of pressure, he might have realized that his trainee had not properly operated the valve. With his last drop of energy, he might have pushed by and under the chief, trying to get to the critical valve. If so, we would have found his body near the valve. The chief might have been pushed to safety.

Only one person knows for sure.

He was probably hung over at the time.

Third investigation. Well, not really an investigation. This is more of a story. The two investigations discussed above, along with several other incidents in which alcoholism played a major role, all occurred in our organization over the space of only a few months. Finally it hit home to us that alcohol abuse had been a factor in nearly every one of our major problems.

So we decided to do something about it. We announced an amnesty program of rehabilitation for anyone who wanted help—we would guarantee the person would be returned to his exact same position and job after therapy, or the person could go somewhere less stressful.

This thoughtful, considerate policy got exactly one taker out of a work force of fifteen thousand people.

Next we went on the road. We put on a dog-and-pony show for all the supervisors, talking about how we were not going to tolerate alcoholism, and that supervisors who did tolerate it were no longer going to be supervisors.

We also provided some assistance by giving the supervisors the names of men whom our investigations over the past few months had identified as having alcohol problems.

This less enlightened, dictatorial policy of threats resulted in a dozen or two men being sent to alcohol rehabilitation—all senior officers or senior enlisted men in leadership positions.

We learned two things from this experience:

The alcoholics we identified were all senior men with outstanding performance records. They were men who had been competent for so long that they were no longer closely supervised (supervisors are always spending eighty percent of their time with the bottom twenty percent of their people). Thus supervisors really don't notice when one of their superstars drinks a bit. They effectively never look at him.

This does not mean that all alcoholics are superior people. What it does mean is that the only alcoholic likely to get through the corporate system is the very exceptional one or, more likely, the one who develops his alcohol problem relatively late in his professional life. We catch the dirt bags and the ones who get into fights or don't come to work on time when they are young and beginning work. That is the time when they have no one junior to cover up for them.

The alcoholics who have an effect on the organization are not the young ones. Young ones don't have authority or responsibility. The alcoholics who affect an organization are the ones who have responsibility for other people. They are usually senior people. "Senior" is another way of saying they will be difficult to identify.

Secondly, when you deal with an alcoholic, you are on your own. Neither the alcoholic nor his family will thank you. The grateful alcoholic and thankful spouse exist only in novels.

So don't expect thanks.

You also won't get any help in making the decision.

The alcoholic isn't going to help. If he were at the stage where he was asking for help, then he wouldn't be a problem to identify. If he is not yet at that stage, then he is still in the process of denying he has a problem. An alcoholic is never going to help you help him. He's a fighter and an actor. He's good at both. He is going to fight you every inch of the way.

Commanders also get no help from those services or groups from which they might expect assistance. Those groups (religion-affiliated, rehabilitation-affiliated, or general social service–oriented) are all exclusively interested in the individual. They want to do what is best for him.

The commander is interested in the individual, but the commander also bears responsibility for the performance of the organization and is interested in the people the alcoholic is affecting.

The bottom line is that a decision has to be made, and that decision is a command determination. You are never going to get consensus on this one. Any decision about an alcoholic is inevitably a lonely decision.

To return to the story. After we had been through about a year of this trauma of recognizing alcoholism and alcoholics as a problem and gone out and scoured the organization both to eliminate and to help the alcoholics, we sat around and complimented ourselves on how well we had done. We had learned the lessons. We had learned how to handle the alcohol problem.

At the time, one of our coworkers was a woman whose husband was a senior person in another part of the organization. We saw her several times a day and saw her husband at least once a day, and often more frequently. We saw both of them socially and professionally.

She was good. Her husband was exceptional. Nice couple. Nice family. They were having some problems with their teenaged boys. Who doesn't? The boys were having loud parties when their parents were gone and the police had been called in several times. Finally both boys had run off to join the Navy.

All the people who worked for her husband liked both her and him. They unanimously praised him. And yet we finally noticed that after six months to a year or so each person working for her husband asked for a transfer.

Why?

Each transfer had a different reason. All the reasons seemed good.

But why so many? We finally decided to give the best person working for him—a woman supervisor with an exceptional record—the third degree when she came in and asked to move.

"Is he abusing you? Is he making sexual advances?"

"No."

"Is he mean?"

"No."

"Does he drink?"

"No. I just want to move to be nearer my sister."

Months more went by. We reviewed his record. We made an effort to watch the officer more carefully. In casual conversation, the wife talked about how her sons were doing in the Navy. They were finding it hard. One had been admitted for alcohol rehabilitation. Sad. He had gone into rehabilitation on his birthday—his eighteenth.

Two more people asked to be transferred from her husband's division.

We talked to longtime friends of the officer. We talked to old supervisors. No one would come out and say he was an alcoholic. All of them managed to mention in the conversations that he drank a bit.

Finally we put all our suppositions in writing and recommended to the officer's boss that the officer be sent to alcohol rehabilitation. The boss sat on it for a month (he may have been reluctant to pass the recommendation on because his own supervisor was very good friends with the suspected alcoholic). Something else happened, which I don't recall anymore. We went directly to the boss's boss and recommended action.

The man went over to be screened for admission to be treated for alcoholism. They confronted him with the documents we had submitted. He explained all the incidents away. The alcoholism screening counsellor wrote down that the officer was not an alcoholic and should not be sent to treatment or bothered again.

That afternoon his wife came to see me. She explained that she and her husband had both been hurt by the unjust accusations. She explained that her husband's occasional flushed face had been caused by some drugs he was taking to overcome his impotency. She told me that her husband had discarded these drugs down the drain that afternoon. He was no longer giving anyone any cause to suspect him of being an alcoholic! Even if it ruined their marriage! She cried in my room for an hour.

I have never felt worse.

Late that same evening, his wife called my secretary from the hospital. Her husband had gotten drunk and broken her jaw. He had beaten her the way he had often beaten their sons. She told my secretary where to look in their home for the secret medical report. She talked about his car—and his office.

We found the medical report hidden behind the drawer of his nightstand. It documented his advanced case of cirrhosis of the liver. We looked in his car as his wife had suggested. We found the false floorboard in his car, with little styrofoam dividers for half-pints of liquor. All full. We found the file cabinet in his office, with every other folder holding something besides records. We found the beeper system his people had paid for out of their own pockets and installed to call him quickly from the bar when his boss asked for him.

Enough. The officer was on his way to an alcoholic rehabilitation clinic the very next day.

He was out within six hours.

He was out because he had to be rushed to the hospital in a coma. His body could not take the withdrawal of not having alcohol for six hours. He nearly died. He was in a coma for days.

His doctor called me up and yelled at me over the telephone. Why hadn't I done something earlier? Didn't I realize this man had been physically dying? Didn't I care?

He is now a recovering alcoholic and, by all reports, doing an excellent job.

Identifying alcoholics is tough.

This was a pretty large organization we were dealing with. Lots of people, pressure, and problems. Some pretty bad things happen in big organizations. Probably bound to, given the number of different people involved. It was interesting that in the two years we watched, most of the truly egregious things that happened were associated with alcoholism. Even the drug investigation stemmed from the decision by some rehabilitators that they wouldn't report the drug use of known alcohol abusers.

Alcoholics are some of the most destructive people in an organization. Assuming, of course, that you have an effective drug urinalysis program that prevents people from using other drugs. If you don't, then you have to add "drug abusers" to "alcoholics" on this very short list of devastatingly destructive people.

Why include these stories in a book on leadership? Because getting rid of the rot is one of the key responsibilities of any leader. People often become alcoholics or drug abusers after they have become so senior that they have already gotten by most or all of the organizational screening processes that normally pick up aberrant behavior. You don't suddenly get stupid or careless after fifteen years on the job. You are essentially the same person you were at twenty-two, with a little wisdom sprinkled on top. However, someone can slip into becoming an alcoholic or a drug abuser while everyone in the organization still thinks of him as being that superstar he always was.

Organizations don't easily get rid of the alcoholic and drug abuser. Social systems, social groups, and counsellors are of limited help. They usually won't even assist you in seeing the signs of decay unless you are unusually wise and learn how to work with them.

Once you have found the rot, there are going to be a lot of people telling you it is something else. Half your staff is suddenly going to be on annual vacation. The other half is going to be murmuring, "It's not alcoholism, it's apple butter." I know of no touchstone for success. I know of no way to be absolutely sure someone is an alcoholic or drug abuser. I do believe that failure to act on your best convictions is absolutely deadly for the organization.

Sometimes failure to act may be equally deadly for the individual.

# CHAPTER FOURTEEN

# Voting

Some people are exceptional leaders. Most of the rest of us can at least contribute. And we average ones are usually eager. Mention something about leadership and our ears perk up. We're interested in improving.

On the other hand, a few people in leadership positions are downright poor. They never make goals. They alienate people unnecessarily, are unable to understand why, and are resistant to change. They don't appear even to comprehend good leadership concepts. These people are downright destructive to any organization.

They are not just destructive to their own unit or command. When a leader is no good his influence spreads downwind like the smell from a pulp mill. And it is a smell that can't be covered up. Three good leaders can't overcome the impact of one bad one. Peers from other commands watch the poor leader and are ashamed to be wearing the same uniform. Unaffected men see, listen, and talk, and think how it would be if they were transferred "over there" some day. Or to somewhere like "there." Juniors often leave the organization rather than take that chance.

A bad leader in an organization is a malignant cancer. Nothing less.

About now, you are thinking along one of two lines, depending primarily on how long you have been around. If you are just starting your career, you are probably thinking, Well, if everybody realizes that, why doesn't someone take a sharp knife and cut them out? It's obvious who those bastards are.

And if you are a bit older you may be saying to yourself, Doesn't he realize how hard it is to judge someone's leadership capability? We need every good man we can get. Besides, how sure are you, really, that one bad apple affects the entire barrel? We don't run this man's organization on old wives' tales.

Why is the absence of leadership so obvious to the people being led, and at the same time so difficult for seniors to evaluate? How much difference does leadership really make?

In the nuclear submarine business our most limited asset is good people. We recruit exceptional people and spend a great deal of time training them. We cannot run nuclear submarines without good people. It is not at all misleading to say that the capability of our submarine force is directly dependent upon the quality of our people.

People are our most limiting asset. We have recognized that for years.

If we break a valve, we can buy a new one.

If we don't have enough qualified supervisors with five or ten years of experience, we cannot buy our way out. There is no shortcut. It takes five years at sea on a nuclear submarine to get a nuclear-trained officer with five years of seagoing submarine experience.

Because the submarine force needs to keep people, and recognizes that, it follows logically that our best leadership talents should be addressed to keeping men in the submarine force. But we have had only mixed success.

Why? Good question. Shows you are paying attention. To continue. . . .

Once upon a time, there was a wardroom full of unhappy submarine officers. For three years they had had the same commanding officer and the same executive officer. The commanding officer was a smart, very remote commander. He stayed in his room a great deal. In three years he never praised one officer—for anything. He even had a couple of good ones. The executive officer was a very active, hands-on individual. The commanding officer let him run the ship. In the three years these two were teamed, not one officer on that ship chose to remain in the submarine service.

One officer committed suicide. At least a dozen resigned. Not one completed his tour there and went on to another ship. At the end of the first three years, every officer on board (except the commanding officer, the executive officer, and one iconoclast) had formally announced his intention to resign. That would have put the losses at about twenty for this one ship.

Finally the executive officer left and a new officer reported to take his place. He also was a hands-on individual. Very smart. Very effective. However, there was one difference. He wasn't a son of a bitch. In the next four months all the officers on board who had submitted their resignation letters (you had to announce your intentions a year in advance in those days) retracted those letters. Subsequently, every officer aboard made the submarine force a thirty-year career.*

Was this just chance? Was the original executive officer simply doing his job of enforcing discipline? Was leadership involved? Was the lack of retention the fault of the executive officer? Or was the commanding officer at fault for failing to remove or redirect the executive officer?

Interesting question. I thought about it for years. Maybe these were just special circumstances aboard just one ship.

Ten years later the opportunity came to study officer retention on all the ships in one of the submarine forces.**

Well, to do a pseudoscientific study, you need to understand your assumptions. It is accepted dogma that the ship reflects the character of the commanding officer. This should be particularly true for a submarine, as submarine officers have longer command tours than those of other warfare specialties.† Take that as the first assumption. Then, add a corollary assumption that men who have been in command for longer than a year have eradicated all good and bad vestiges of their predecessors.††

---

* As we are doing subsequentlies, subsequently the commanding officer was hospitalized for the treatment of alcoholism, and the executive officer, who had the same problem, was ordered into treatment for abusing his wife.

** The United States submarines are divided into Atlantic and Pacific forces, commanded by different staffs. This appears to lead to inefficiencies, but actually produces so much competition for improvements that it has served the country very well.

† At the time of this story, the submarine commanding officer tour lasted nearly four years, with the surface officer command tour about two years and the aviation command tour a year.

†† My observation is that this process actually takes about three months to lose the good things the predecessor was doing, and about six months to overcome the poorer practices that were in vogue.

That's it. Two assumptions. Now, for the study we simply looked at each commanding officer in the force who had been in command for at least two years and counted up how many of his officers had resigned. Then we compared those numbers with the total number of officers in the force who had resigned in the same two years.

Amazing! Ninety percent of the officer resignations in the previous two years were from ten percent of our units.

If our assumptions were true, five commanding officers had caused the resignations of more than thirty-five junior officers. Each of the five commanders had at least six resignations from his wardroom. None of the rest of the fifty submarine crews had more than two resignations.

We worked out the statistics. You can do the same. There was little likelihood that the numbers were due to chance.

We looked at the five ships. The ships all happened to report to one boss. He said that he couldn't believe he would have missed any big problems in the ships.

With some urging, he looked again. "Now that you mention it, hadn't noticed it earlier, but these ships do not look good."

Ten years later,* there was belated confirmation that these particular officers had not been good leaders. Four of the five failed to be promoted to the next higher rank. The four were among the very, very few nuclear-trained submarine officers in their peer group not promoted. Obviously they were in the bottom ten percent. Perhaps they were unsatisfactory.

Ten years more went by. We looked anew. This time the sample size was half the force. In the last two years before the evaluation, there had been twenty-eight resignations from twenty-four ships. Surprise, again! Twenty-one resignations were from only three ships!

We looked at these three ships a little more carefully. When compared with all the other submarines, two were dead last in cleanliness and material conditions. No other submarine was close.

We went to sea with them. When compared with their fellow commanding officers, none of the three commanding officers seemed comfortable with the decisions and actions required of the man in command. One did everything himself, never permitting anyone to act

---

* It is difficult to become a seer without longevity. Need to be able to point out where you were right. Need to be around long enough to figure out what happened.

without his personal supervision. One let his officers do whatever they felt best, appearing not even to involve himself in the tough decisions that had to be made. The third commander was negligent in his professional knowledge of engineering (which is an unavoidable and significant part of submarining). He avoided even walking in the engineering spaces.*

Within the next six months each of the three commanding officers had been involved in a casualty or decision so egregious it resulted in him being relieved of his command.**

If you are familiar with Navy retention programs, you are probably asking yourself—what about enlisted retention? Did it mirror the officer problems?

Nope. Neither exactly nor approximately. Some of the ships that had awful officer retention had very good enlisted retention. This wasn't a real surprise. We have always had a bureaucratic problem with this mismatch. Seldom do we give the annual E for excellence to the ship with the highest enlisted retention. All of us who have looked at the retention numbers and compared them with other things we know about the ships know that the relative enlisted retention standing of a ship does not faithfully reflect the relative capability of that ship or the leadership of its commanding officer.

Why don't we use officer retention numbers? Can't—or at least it's hard. The number of officer losses is a small number. You often have to average them over a couple of years to begin to see something. On the other hand, we do have enlisted retention figures. We have ten times as many enlisted people as officers. In a year, you can get enough enlistment decisions to be able to calculate some percentages for every unit in the Navy. Everyone in the Navy and Department of Defense keeps track of the enlisted retention. Each submarine force commander issues a monthly message in which he reports how each unit is doing in enlisted retention. Which submarines have gone up. Which have gone down. No one usually tracks officer retention by unit.

---

* Although he had received very high grades in the appropriate disciplines in Navy schools and on tests!
** One drove his ship into a submerged reef. One demonstrated a lack of professional judgment in deciding to operate his ship with a known material casualty. One hit another ship.

Why does officer retention reflect commanding officer leadership capabilities, and enlisted retention not? I'm unsure. There are some theories, however.

The most common belief is that the enlisted man can reenlist for a specified benefit, such as being assigned earlier to another submarine or to a school or to shore duty. These actions frequently result in the man getting off the submarine and out of his current situation. Officers are not normally permitted to get away from one particular ship early.

I'm not convinced this supposition is valid. I think the reason is more basic. The enlisted man looks for leadership, and for his self-image, to his leading petty officer, or division chief, or division officer. Maybe as far as his department head. He may see the commanding officer once every couple of days. Often less.

The officers aboard a submarine are in constant contact with the commanding officer. They eat together, watch movies together, go on liberty together, and certainly work together. All the officers are supposed to aspire to be commanding officers. They aren't working to be helmsmen, or engineers, or even executive officers, they are working to be commanding officers. When the commanding officer is not very good, or very nice, or very comfortable being in charge, what kind of self-image does that give the junior officer?

You can't keep all the officers you recruit. You don't even want to keep them all. But the submarine force has to retain the hearts and minds of the great majority of the accessions. In the long run, the officer retention rate is a good rough gauge of the commanding officer's leadership. Given the number of people on a submarine who are trying very hard to make the submarine run right (and thereby often effectively disguising the shortcomings of the commanding officer), poor officer retention may be the senior supervisor's first bellwether of trouble.*

I hope this discussion has not been depressing to young officers and executives. I have not meant to imply that all is lost if you are a young officer or executive working for poor leaders. Not at all. In fact,

* Please note that this does not mean to say that we shouldn't closely watch enlisted retention. We need to retain our highly trained people; and enlisted retention rates, and changes therein, may tell us many useful things about policy, relative deficits in pay and benefits, etc. We should just not be terribly surprised if it doesn't tell us anything about the commanding officer's leadership.

you are very much in luck! You are in a much better learning situation than your peer on another ship.

Working for a poor leader is inevitably better for the young executive. First of all, working with a poor leader is much more instructive than working for a good one. A poor leader will irritate you so much you will spend days thinking about what he does, how he does it, and exactly why it is wrong. You will inevitably learn a great deal, even if it is just the golden rule of treating people the way you would like to be treated. No bad leader observes this rule, so you will at least pick this one up.

On the other hand, with a good leader you probably wouldn't even notice lots of what he was doing.

Second, when working for a poor leader, you will probably learn to work harder. A poor leader makes it more difficult to do anything well. To do the same job as your peer in another unit you will have to expend a great deal more time and effort. Good! Just think how much those learned work habits will help you accomplish when you finally work for a good leader!

Third, working for a poor leader stresses you more. It makes you develop your capabilities. Anyone can work for a good leader. It takes real stamina to work for a dolt.

A poor leader can make his whole command one big leadership lesson.

Unfortunately, from your boss's supervisor's perspective, there is no such silver lining. Poor leadership is never worth a damn to the organization. Poor leadership always gets less from people. Any people. Poor leadership also produces problems. The problems don't wear signs saying that they are the product of poor leadership. Instead, they are disguised as something else (alcoholism, discipline infractions, broken or unreliable equipment) to make it harder to trace the problem back. And, precisely because the supervisor is not a peer or junior, and doesn't spend months in the environment, poor leadership is tough for the supervisor to evaluate. Because poor leaders are often particularly nice to their seniors, it is difficult for the supervisor to identify immediately when leadership is so poor that the employment or services of that executive should be terminated.

Bad leaders are always left in place too long.

The supervisor should remember one thing. I call it my silver rule. Poor officer retention is prima facie evidence of poor leadership. If people are not happy, they vote with their feet.

# CHAPTER FIFTEEN

## Walking

Someone once told me that IBM has a company management policy they call management by walking around, or MBWA. If so, count me as one in favor of that policy and term. I, too, think that MBWA is the best way to run an organization.

It is frankly startling how positively you affect people by walking around the work area. There seem to be two factors operating. One is the old Hawthorne Experiment principle.* When management is just *seen* and appears interested, productivity often soars.

The second inevitable result of walking around is that you affect the flow of information. That may not sound important, but for a leader, the stallion named Information always runs neck and neck in the feature race with the mare Insight. When you walk around people either manage to tell you things to your face, or they make sure you "overhear" at least part of what they would like you to take in. Walking around is chumming the organization for information.

The information received does not necessarily carry with it any special cachet of validity. The bits are no better or worse than any

---

* Widely known as one of the first time and motion studies, in which the amount of light available in the work space was varied to determine the effect on productivity. When the light was reduced, productivity went up. When the light was increased, productivity went up. Finally it was recognized that the effect of the light making the job harder or easier was not nearly as important to productivity as the attention the workers were receiving.

other raw inputs. In fact, it is the wise man who realizes that very little of what he hears while walking around is either true, important, worth pursuing, or any combination of the three. Walking the work area is like rotating farmland. The farmer plants alfalfa for the same reason the leader accepts any inputs. Not from an expectation of a particularly valuable crop, but because all inputs, gathered by other than normal means, whether true or false, help mulch the organizational soil.

Random informational tidbits from the field also serve other purposes. They help you evaluate morale. They help determine how well the organization understands its goals, and how your guidance is filtering down and being interpreted. Perhaps even more importantly, samples from the field give you some insight into how well your people are doing at evaluating information and choosing whether or not to send it up the line.

No matter how useless the information you get from walking around, think of the hours spent as insurance fees paid to prevent the worst fate that can befall a leader in this modern world—capture!

The organization needs you making decisions that are earmarked with your own maturity and judgment. Neither you nor the organization want you making what are essentially only pseudodecisions—decisions that are inevitable and unavoidable, given the incomplete or slanted information you have been permitted to learn by your staff or trusted executive assistant. You are no value to anyone if you have been captured by your staff.

Given the high price of maintaining a personal guard of eunuchs these days, the least expensive option is to buy anticapture insurance. You can't find that insurance listed in a brochure, or through electronic mail, or by doing anything while sitting in an office at the end of an information funnel. Anticapture policies aren't sold door to door. This insurance can be bought only while walking around.

There are also the more conventional rewards that come from walking your experience around the workplace. I once was on a submarine that was undergoing an overhaul in a shipyard. The shipyard had overcommitted itself. It simply had much too much work for its work force. The overhaul on our ship was surely going to end some day, but just as surely it was not going to be by the day that had been contracted for. The delay was costing the shipyard and the Navy money over budget, and it was also keeping some sailors from going to sea. In cases like these, where all parties are interested in speeding up the schedule, you have to be particularly careful about maintaining quality.

During the overhaul, as the delays had become apparent, I had been making myself particularly unpleasant with the guy in charge of the shipyard, and had even been talking with his boss about the shipyard's inability to maintain a schedule. About three o'clock one morning, I was walking around my submarine. As my wife and I had just come home from a trip, I was not wearing my uniform, just an old sweater over my shirt and trousers. While ambling around smoking, I saw someone off by himself welding on a critical piece. I stopped to watch and he stopped to talk.

He pushed up his welding mask and said, "I can't believe they have me doing this. I don't even know how to weld on this goddamn kind of steel. Have you got another smoke on you?" I flipped a Winston out of my pack and held it up to his lips so he wouldn't have to remove his canvas welding gloves, and he continued, talking around the cigarette.

"I don't even have the right rods." He took a deep drag to light the butt from the match I held, nodded his thanks and looked me in the eyes. "This is submarine steel, and I'm a trash-iron welder. I'm supposed to be working over on that big freighter on the other side of the yard, welding up that hole they cut in her side."

He looked away from me, back toward his job. "My boss says that no one will ever know, as long as I finish tonight. He says we got to get this done to keep that bastard captain off our backs. He told me to finish this job, no questions asked. Now, ain't that a bitch?"

And he shook his head, and heaved his shoulders wearily, spat the cigarette out of his mouth, ground it carefully into the deck, turned, and went back to his welding.

Did he know that I was that bastard?

Maybe. Probably not.

Was he comfortable doing a job wrong? Was he happy about doing something which he professionally thought might possibly break and hurt someone? Absolutely not. Most people are very uncomfortable when they are doing something they know is wrong.

Would he have finished the job if I hadn't stopped by?

Sure. The work paid well. His boss had told him to. He needed the job. He couldn't say anything unless someone walked by—without people thinking he was deliberately ratting on them. But when someone walked by and gave him a cigarette, he couldn't very well snub them, could he? He wasn't looking for trouble. Who of his peers or supervisors could blame him? "Any dumb son of a bitch could tell from the color of the arc I was using the wrong welding rod for stainless!"

Would our crew had found out if I hadn't been walking around? Probably not. One weld looks a lot like another. We wouldn't have known until it broke. When it broke we might have been far from the shipyard. We might have been far from any help. We might have been deep under the sea.

Informal, valuable information exchanges take place every day in organizations when supervisors are walking around.

There is another significant advantage to having leaders walk around the workplace. Because he can't physically be in two separate places, when a supervisor is walking around he or she isn't spending time in his/her office reviewing or asking for another useless piece of paper. Terrific! Anything that reduces paper shuffling contributes to the more efficient operation of an organization.

Most paper exists only to establish a legal trail of who was or was not clearly (usually only somewhat clearly) wrong. That kind of paper can be kept by clerks.*

It is amazing how many people are interested in establishing records that they can use later on to prove that they advised their boss to buy Zebra stock at 22½.

Doesn't matter.

Even if the stock rose to 126, it doesn't matter. If you were unable to convince your boss to buy earlier, you failed. You may have been prescient, but you were not convincing. Why do you want a document to prove that? When the stock hits 126 your boss is not going to ask for the file that clearly proves you told him so.

If instead it was you who decided not to buy at 22½, and the person who talked you out of it isn't emblazoned in your mind, then you can

---

* Which doesn't mean that records should not be kept, but that one should recognize why one is keeping a record and the level of effort that should be involved, and assign responsibilities appropriately.

chalk that one up to your own error account. Don't waste time trying to pin it on some other slug.

What use are most records, except as full-employment incentives for lawyers? If the organization fails everyone is at fault. Did it matter which Japanese military leaders advised their government not to start a war with the United States? Didn't prevent any of the deaths in the Pacific. Loss records are of no interest to doers. So why did you keep them? Records of successes that don't give the credit to your boss for wins are equally worthless. One thing you can always bank on. Your boss knows he was responsible for success. "The moving finger writes; and having writ, moves on." Move with it.

In addition to paper written and kept by clerks, there is another common type of rag bond. This is paper that exists to keep the supervisor from having to walk away from his desk and come face to face with a problem. Leaders who shouldn't be leaders are seemingly always asking for the ritual sacrifice of another tree.

Don't fall into this trap. It may look good and brief well, but it is a poor way to lead. How do you prevent it? First, when you have thought of a new paper system that will improve efficiency, always reconsider. Discard all those new systems that don't result in the replacement of more paper than they cause.

Then arbitrarily discard most of the new systems that successfully pass this test. Don't institute them after all. You always underestimate how much work they would initiate. Instead, along with them throw away the paper they would have replaced. Now get up from the desk and walk around the workplace.

Frequent walking around keeps a leader from becoming a paper tiger. Walking around is the activator that starts the random process that will inevitably match the leader up against hard questions, and people who are not happy, and people not in the palace guard who would like to be, and people who think the palace guard stinks, or is dishonest, or stupid—or think it is the palace guard's boss who is dishonest or stupid. Sooner or later someone you meet walking around will say it in French so plain that you or any leader can understand.

People who don't like to work on life's real problems, or don't like to get the hems of their robes dirty, tend to stay in their offices and invent or perpetuate paper systems. It is only natural.

Walking around keeps a leader from giving in to that natural tendency to be comfortable. MBWA is a valuable leadership tool.

*    *    *

If you remember high school geometry, there were often corollaries to established theorems. Management by walking around implies leadership through opinion sampling and close observation of selected evolutions. There is another, equally useful type of MBWA. I call it management by walking away.*

Management by walking away is a tool for managing people who are not performing known and routine actions. It is for those less structured situations—those when there is no known good answer. The principal advantage to this style is that a leader will often get more from the members of his group if he gets out of their hair and lets them worry the problem.

There are drawbacks to this method. You have to decide if the cost is worth the gain. In many cases the leader is trying to get people to think of new solutions. He is willing to accept the short-term inefficiencies that often result from less closely supervised efforts.

In other scenarios the supervisor is pragmatically accepting that some individuals produce much more when they are operating in a relatively unconstrained environment.

There are other advantages to walking away. Not only do you get more original thinking from the group when your shadow isn't

---

* As you may have noticed, I use the terms "management" and "leadership" nearly interchangeably. I have never been able to separate one from the other. Tools that serve managers well seem to be equally effective in the hands of men who call themselves leaders. Some people, and Admiral Rickover professed to be one, believed that leadership was the only valid effort for naval officers. The implication was that "management" efforts were useless. Many arguments ensued from his pronouncements. I never could quite follow the discussion. My best guess was that Admiral Rickover believed that too many intelligent people try to study "management" in the classroom rather than getting their hands dirty by practicing leadership in the work environment.

This makes sense, especially given his special problems. Admiral Rickover was trying to wean students away from the ivy walls of academe. He was recruiting for the nuclear submarine program a group of people who were eligible for (and often inclined towards) all sorts of postgraduate studies. But he didn't need people smoking pipes and studying in some room at Harvard, he needed them at sea serving in submarines. Therefore he encouraged lifelong self-study, as he had practiced himself. He had observed that a man could study the social sciences on his own much easier than it was possible to understand mathematics and physics by himself. He therefore urged people (at least he once took forty minutes to urge me) to use their college time (when they had the aid of an instructor) for the hard sciences, and pursue the social sciences, such as "management," concurrent with their life's work.

hummingbirding nearby, you also have time to expand your personal span of control, and you have more opportunity to develop and evaluate young leadership. In addition, by putting some space between you and your office, you will be better able to think, unbiased by perceived "facts" and independent of the pressure of day-to-day crises.

Once upon a time I was assigned aboard a submarine that had been operated without adequate time set aside for maintenance. The submarine was a mess. There were problems with equipment, people, and paperwork. There wasn't one area under the paint that wasn't rotten to the touch. Everyone had finally recognized the problem, and there were lots of people working hard to fix the condition of the submarine and bring it up to standard. As you might expect, everyone was interested in how we were doing. In fact, they were so interested that we were tasked to provide weekly progress briefings to the local area admiral.

Would we be ready to go again in two weeks? Three? Four?

Hard to tell. Only thing we knew for sure is that we weren't making much forward progress. In fact, we were still in the process of discovering more things wrong. Each week we uncovered more things that were broken than we had fixed the week before. The pressure of a weekly briefing for an admiral just added to our burden. We had our heads down leaning into the traces so hard that we didn't notice we were still sliding backwards. When we did notice, because every inch lost was so painful, we didn't dare look up and chance losing another foot. We had no idea where we were going.

Finally a senior officer* walked through the ship. He made one slight change. He changed the periodicity of the reports. He cancelled the weekly report. He asked us to tell him how we were doing in a year.

Interesting! He had decided we were capable, were trying, and would root out and fix the problems we found. So he left us alone.

We stopped and stepped back. Took a deep breath. And saw more problems. Hell, it was worse than we had thought! But it was up to us to fix.

---

* He was only a captain at the time, although later, not surprisingly, he served as a four-star admiral.

A year later, they gave us all praise and medals. Everyone was amazed that we had been so perceptive. We had found and corrected problems no one had suspected. Everyone was amazed that we had thought of such original fixes. Everyone was amazed we had worked so hard.

Self-motivation is a powerful mover. However, just like a baby elephant, it needs adequate growing room.*

Second example. The United States Navy is currently divided into four operating fleets. The Seventh Fleet is the group of sailors, marines, ships, airplanes, and submarines that steams the waters roughly between Hawaii and Africa. The admiral who commands that fleet has significant political and social responsibilities in the many countries in that area, in addition to his responsibility for directing the operation of the fleet. How does he do it?

Several different ways. Each admiral must, of course, operate in a manner he finds comfortable. Some have remained close to the flagship on which the fifty-man staff was located, the ship from which the admiral would probably choose to fight, if events so required. These men have chosen to work daily with their staff, handling the routine and not-so-routine events of that part of the world. Other admirals chose to travel far and wide, communicating daily with the staff but personally visiting the flagship only infrequently. The first method is more usual. Why would you do the second? What do you gain by not being with your staff?

A lot.

There is a significant advantage to looking at the same problems the staff is examining, untouched by knowledge of the specifics. The leader's image of the problem isn't contaminated by some misreported fact. The leader's identification of the critical aspects isn't influenced by the personalities of the people who provided the information. He

---

* Much, much later I realized that in place of us making periodic reports, he had inserted a trusted agent who made periodic reports on our progress. Didn't matter. He had officially recognized the large scope of the problem and turned off the pressure for short-term results. Asking for short-term results often prevents long-term progress.

also isn't distracted by other less important events or routine crises. The leader still receives his staff's best position, but he gets it largely without emotion, in the black and white of the printed word. And he retains the independence of his own evaluation. Appealing gains—all achieved by walking away.

And the leader has retained the ability to feed his own ideas back into the staff. At the same time, through his presence, he is affecting people and events thousands of miles away from his primary staff. He has achieved a much larger span of control, even though he might prefer the word *influence* to the word *control* in this context. Interesting.

Last example. Given the physical difficulty of communicating with a submarine and the submarine's stealth ability, we have found it best to employ the submarine off by itself in the deep blue sea, administratively armed only with broad guidance.

As a direct result of the submarine crew being unable to communicate stealthily back to its boss, the boss is reluctant to give the submarine crew very specific orders that might be dangerously misunderstood. Instead, his superior provides the submarine commanding officer no orders, or some rather general guidance and a few direct orders. The superior then waits until the submarine commanding officer comes home to ask him how and what he actually accomplished. Because of the consequent great latitude of action and responsibility, a submariner's most fulfilling experience is acting as commanding officer during a deployment.

A deployment—no other ships around, sometimes thousands of miles from the nearest friendly face, no communications home for months— is an exhilarating challenge. Bringing the submarine safely home, with its mission accomplished, is emotionally and professionally satisfying. Intensely so. It is one reason the submarine force is able to attract and keep good people.

The challenge also rather quickly tends to separate the sheep from the ducks. Some officers do unexpectedly well. Others, often equally unexpectedly, find reasons not to succeed. The Navy gets an accurate and early evaluation of real leadership capability by letting these young men perform on their lonesome out in the great seas. It is a classic case of providing an exceptional environment for leadership development by walking away.

Let's assume that you are interested in the advantages of leadership by walking away. You probably have two questions. What do I do with my time if I'm not always closely supervising somebody, and how do I get my boss to walk away from managing me?

The first part is easy. If you do not have a better use for your time, then you shouldn't be "walking away." It is not a management style for everyone. It is not even a management style appropriate for all supervisory tasks. Many jobs, especially the junior management ones (such as the division officers' aboard submarines) are intended to be close supervision jobs. The supervisor in these jobs is in the process of learning the basic building blocks of leadership and people management. Every day he is learning something new and putting the knowledge to practice. He should be walking around, not walking away.

On the other hand, several years later, when you have learned all the jobs involved in a particular line of work and have proved your ability, how do you best use your experience and judgment? Who in your organization is doing the original thinking, conception, and correlation? Who is worrying about why you are building widgets instead of building something else, rather than worrying about how to build widgets more efficiently?

Often no one. No one has the time. Very few have the necessary experience. Even fewer have the required judgment.

For senior leaders and managers who have earned the right to establish their own work boundaries, I have one rule of thumb. If you are comfortable doing your job you are not taking on hard enough challenges. Anyone at your level of management should be able to think of several problems that you would address *if* you but had the time, which *only* you could do. Heck, given the problems you have, who could be comfortable?

If you can't think of anything to do, try walking away anyway. It is still a good management technique. If you can't think, at least take up golf. Your people (especially your deputy) have lots of positive things they might do if only you weren't always hovering around.

So much for how you might use any time you gain from walking away. The more interesting question is how you get your boss to walk away and give you some time to catch up. If he really walked away, you might have the time to institute that new program you have been thinking of. . . .

If you truly want to be managed on a loose rope, you need to make your boss feel that he can see through your organization as clearly as a first-year medical student looks through the skeleton hanging in the corner of the anatomy classroom.

Your boss has to believe you aren't hiding anything. Which should be fine with you. You want your boss to value you for your judgment, your ability to get extra performance from your people, and the insight of your philosophy. You aren't interested in suddenly surprising him with anything—even increased output. Surprises are always a no-no. For everybody.

One way to increase the length of your rope is to set up deliberate, informal lines of communication between your subordinates and staff members and your boss's staff. Might as well. If you don't want them, they will be established secretly anyway. Besides, approved informal lines of communication can serve your needs as well as your superior's. To begin with, approved informal lines of communication mean that there will be fewer inadvertent surprises. And, because you don't care what information is exchanged, the approved existence of these communications links underlines the fact that your organization has nothing to hide.

Secondly, by making your own staff open, you gain access to your boss's staff. Only streets are one-way. Informal lines of communication work forth and back. With an open staff, you now have nonthreatening, indirect access to his staff. If you have taught your staff well, they will influence their counterparts with your philosophy. Truth sells. If you have a good philosophy, there should be few important bureaucratic battles you won't win.

Because you are not hiding anything, your boss can afford to walk away.

Q.E.D.

# CHAPTER SIXTEEN

## Integrity

In many large organizations there is a contingent of thought that the contest usually goes to the man willing to sail closest to the fine line drawn between truth and less-than-that. Some self-styled pragmatists regale audiences with stories that might lead a novice to believe that success is the province of only the most gnarled and least scrupulous bureaucratic battlers.

That has not been my experience. In fact, I am concerned that such tripe might be discouraging to the men who would be the very leaders we need. No matter what you have heard, personal integrity is in itself an excellent armament. There is always room at the top for the honest man.

Truth sells itself.

Lies deed your soul to the devil.

Once upon a time a lady brought suit against the Navy because she said that our submarine had been going too fast when it passed her own boat in the river. She further alleged that the bow wave resulting from our submarine's "clearly excessive" speed caused her to injure her back. Some water areas have speed limits, just like school zones. For instance, the speed limit where the alleged incident had taken place was nine knots.

The old unprovable back problem suit! Almost as common as traffic accident whiplash claims. From a lady with a history of hypochondria! The Navy defense lawyers interviewed eighteen people from the submarine. All of them said that the ship was going at or below the permitted speed.

The Navy lawyers then asked each of the eighteen people how big the wake from the ship was at the submarine's fastest speed. Each of the men gave an answer, with the answers varying nearly inversely with the seniority of the individual providing the information. (The captain said in his pretrial affidavit that the wake was no more than a few feet high; the most junior seaman thought that the wake crested at nearly thirty feet.)

The Navy lawyers needed someone who could be a witness for the Navy to establish that the ship was professionally operated. The commanding officer couldn't come. He was going to be deployed on another submarine when the case came to court. The executive officer was scheduled to be present, but the Navy lawyers thought he might not be the very best witness as he had also been acting as navigator, and although the executive officer maintained that the submarine had been going only nine or ten knots, expert reconstruction of the track indicated that the ship had been doing at least fifteen.

As a last resort, the Navy lawyers located the third senior officer and decided to use him as a witness. There were a couple of problems with using him as an expert witness for the Navy. First of all, although he was the senior officer aboard who physically stood watches on the submarine's bridge, he freely admitted he had no idea how high the bow wave crested. Secondly, the third officer had been standing the engineering watch at the time, and his engineering records established the ship's speed at about eighteen knots at the time of the incident. However, he was the best Navy witness available, so the third officer was pressed into service.

The trial started. The civilian attorneys spent some time with the third officer. He was steadfast that although he probably should, he did not know how high the bow wave crested. The attorneys pointed out that all the officers and even the most inexperienced seaman aboard had provided statements in which they stated how high the wave crested. Why didn't he know? They banged him about for a while. The third officer admitted he probably should have known, but that he had not. He could only guess. The court wanted facts. They did not want any guesses.

The third officer looked d–u–m–b! It was embarrassing. Everyone in the courtroom altered his gaze.

The attorneys next turned their attention to the executive officer. He was called to the stand and sworn in. He did know. He was certain that the bow wave crested, just as the commanding officer had said, at only a few, probably about two to four, feet high. He couldn't explain the excessive speed shown in the engineering record and the track reconstruction, but he was sure the ship had not exceeded nine knots with the commanding officer on the bridge.

The civilian attorneys spent the better part of the morning getting the executive officer to repeat his story in many different ways. After three hours, it was cemented in the court's mind. Even if he wanted to at some future time, the executive officer would never be able to back away from his testimony credibly.

Then they turned the lights out in the courtroom and showed a (heretofore undisclosed) home movie taken by the plaintiff's sister from the plaintiff's sister's boat, which showed the plaintiff posing for the camera leaning against the cabin of her boat, and a submarine suddenly appearing and going by in the background, with the bow wave from the submarine rising quickly up to about fifteen feet, causing the plaintiff's boat suddenly to pitch violently, and the plaintiff to be thrown up in the air and come down with her back across the cabin railing.

Even without sound it hurt.

The Navy attorneys asked for a recess and settled the claim in the hall. Gave her everything she had asked for.

Looking dumb is oodles better than being dishonest.

Funny thing. The commanding officer had personally ordered the excessive speed. The commanding officer was locally famous for his impatience and disregard of rules. The commanding officer had hated the executive officer and had made sure everyone knew it.

The executive officer was forced out of the submarine force.

Next.

Once upon a time a supply officer went in to talk to his commanding officer in private about how to make their wardroom mess the best one in the shipyard.

The commanding officer had told the supply officer that he wanted him to use his initiative to make the noon meal one that would induce all the officers to eat on the ship. As they were in overhaul, the officers could eat wherever they liked. The commanding officer wanted them to prefer to eat together. He had an ulterior motive. He intended to use the discussions at the meal as an officer training forum. The commanding officer believed in the old submarine dictum that the difference between the officers and the chiefs is noon meal (which the officers eat with the commanding officer as they listen to him).

The supply officer made progress each week. Within two months the meals were a great success. The wardroom officers appeared to enjoy the social-professional occasion. There was nearly one hundred percent attendance.

Unfortunately, after a few more weeks the supply officer found he was losing money on the meals (a no-no). After another week or two to check his data, the supply officer moseyed into the commanding officer's office and told him that they could continue the very successful meals, but only by permitting the supply officer a little leeway in how much was surveyed* for each meal. He also told the commanding officer how much he had enjoyed taking the commanding officer's sons fishing with him the previous Sunday afternoon. And how much he and his wife had appreciated the commanding officer's wife finding the supply officer's wife a job the previous week.

The commanding officer told him his sons had been quite excited about the fishing trip. He thanked the supply officer again for taking his sons with him for the day. The commanding officer then thought for a moment and called his two most senior officers into the office, turned to the supply officer, and recapitulated for those two officers what he understood the supply officer to have said. The supply officer nodded. Then the commanding officer said, "You would certify that the vegetables were spoiled and discarded, but then actually use them to make the wardroom meals better?"

"Yes, sir. To balance the accounts."

"It would be at most a few dollars a meal?"

"Never more than ten, sir."

"You probably have heard about it being done on other ships?"

"Oh, yes, sir. All the time."

And then the commanding officer, with his two most senior of-

---

* Surveying is how you account for waste due to rotting vegetables and so on. The ship has only a certain amount of money for each man for each meal. As they usually receive their food from Navy sources, ships are permitted to not account for spoiled food. It is a simple procedure and only a few dollars are normally at stake. The supply officer or one of his assistants certifies the food was spoiled when received, and it is then expensed off the ship's account.

ficers present, explained to the supply officer that not only was he not to do this particular "extra" surveying, but that under no circumstances was he ever even to consider doing anything that wasn't clearly on the right side of the straight and narrow, etcetera, and neither they nor anyone else aboard this ship, etcetera, and how disappointed he was this had even been suggested, etcetera, etcetera.

The commanding officer actually went on much longer than was necessary.

A year later, when the supply officer was accused and then convicted on several hundred counts of theft (apparently his wife wanted nicer things), the fact that there were witnesses to this exchange and verbal admonition was helpful to the investigators in evaluating the command environment. In his plea bargain, the supply officer said that other people in the command had also not done some things exactly right.

When someone does something that is going to land him in jail, the investigators always provide the miscreant an opportunity to roll over and turn in a bigger (more senior) fish—for anything the wrongdoer has seen, heard, or thought might have been illegal. That practice isn't wrong. It is precisely the way good law enforcement works. The risk of a false accusation is one of those risks that go along with being a big fish. The best defense is to be squeaky clean. You never know which of your friends or professional associates will decide to break some law. If you want to be a leader and sleep nights, be publicly, privately, and deliberately squeaky clean.

The investigators decided the supply officer was a liar.

Next.

Let's pause momentarily and talk about what you do when you don't have integrity in an organization. Now, I have never met a truly evil person. From media accounts, it looks as though there are those kinds around, but, as I said, I have never met one. If you are that unlucky, you are on your own. I have read of some luck with a mirror, a cross, and a silver stake, but. . . .

On the other hand, I have met two different types of dishonest people that I do feel qualified to discuss. Neither of these types were basically evil people. Both were good to their mothers, loved apple pie, saluted the flag, and so on. They did some things good people do. But they were not honest.

As a result they were both difficult and unpleasant to work for, work with, or supervise.

Which is a problem. I advocate dealing with people as though they are always honest because I have found that the great majority of people are uncomfortable when placed in a situation in which they are or have to be dishonest. On the other hand, the relatively small number of dishonest people make a leader's job very hard, essentially because their dishonesty makes it tough to evaluate situations accurately. The key is to recognize dishonesty and its root causes. It is not easy.

The most common form of dishonesty is the individual who has rationalized his position to himself so well that he no longer believes he is lying. This man thinks he is absolutely truthful. He can often argue his case with all the fervor of a missionary preaching to the heathen.

The most interesting case I knew was a man who believed anything the second time he said it to himself. When something unpleasant happened and was reported to him, first he said—sort of under his breath—what he wished had happened. Then he would ask if what he wished to have happened hadn't really happened.

If someone didn't definitely stop him right there the game was all over. The next time he spoke, he was just as likely as not to report to his senior that exactly what he wished had happened, had occurred.

Before we recognized this behavior characteristic we were coming into port one afternoon to moor alongside a wooden pier. While the commanding officer was maneuvering the ship alongside, some officers were escorting a senior officer around the engine room to look at a piece of machinery that did not do anything reliably except leak oil profusely. We wanted the senior officer's permission (and money) to replace the machine.

Suddenly the ship hit something. People bounced about like tenpins in a bowling alley. As we tried to avoid falling down we bumped the senior officer, who, being quite short, was pushed against the side of the low-slung machine. Fortunately, with all the oil he easily slid right over the top and was not hurt. Unfortunately, he was wearing his white uniform.

The next cry heard was "Corpsman!"

The medical corpsman came running right at us. And went on by to the men behind us who had come down the ladder from topside. They all had splinters in the exposed skin on their arms and faces. We had hit several of the pier's wooden pilings with our propeller, and everyone topside had at least one splinter from the landing to keep as his own personal talisman. The corpsman was busy with his tweezers and iodine for at least an hour.

We looked topside on our way forward. Parts of six or seven pier timbers were floating in the water behind the submarine. The pier looked as though a billion or so hungry beavers had happened by.

A submarine's propeller, or screw, is a finely balanced device that pushes the submarine quickly through the water with an absolute minimum of noise. The balance tolerances are so fine that the screw is carefully cleaned and polished every time the ship is out of the water. On this particular submarine, which had two of them, the screws projected farther out to the side than the hull of the ship, and thus were particularly vulnerable to accidents like the one that had occurred. We sent divers down to look at the screw on the pier side. The divers reported that three of the blades were damaged. We would have to replace it before we went to sea again. No problem. It was a fairly routine maintenance action for this ship.

We reported the problem to the commanding officer and told him we would put on a new screw tomorrow. He looked at us rather blankly and asked if we had any idea of the probable cause. We stared—and lost our chance.

"I *thought* I saw some wood debris after we pulled in!" he said.

He continued, "I bet there is a sunken log somewhere right in the middle of the mooring slip."

Our mouths were open. Still nothing came forth.

"I bet we hit it on the way in. I thought I felt something. Did you feel anything?"

We nodded.

"I want you to get ship's divers out there and find that log. We need to locate and remove that deadhead* before another submarine also inadvertently hits it."

"Captain, you hit the pier. That's what happened." Our mouths finally were reconnected with our brains.

Too late. He had said it twice. He now believed it. He stared at us as if we had just tried to betray the queen.

---

* A sunken, watersoaked tree. These are common hazards to ships in rivers in some parts of the world. Not here, however, nor anywhere within a thousand miles.

"What? You said you heard it yourself, Mister. Now, get those divers in the water. Neither you nor I are going home until you find that sunken log and blow it up." Then more mildly and reasonably, "We can't let some danger like that go uncorrected. I'll tell the squadron commander what we are doing."

Of course the divers didn't find a thing. After sunset we went back and tried to explain what had happened to the commanding officer one more time. Didn't even faze him.

Finally, shortly before midnight, we put some explosive line-charges around an old concrete block we had found on the bottom. It made a satisfying noise and geyser. The commanding officer wanted to know if there were any more old logs down there. We certified there were not. We all went home. My wife asked me why I was late. I said no reason.

It writes funnier now than it seemed then.

Finally we learned. The commanding officer could have passed any lie detector test ever invented. He believed that whatever was best for him must be exactly the way it had happened.

Interestingly enough, you could deal with him just as though he were honest, because he thought he was. He actually was honest for the instant before his subconscious mind computed what was in his best interest. If you could knife in with your argument then, you got a rational, honest decision. But you had to be quick! If you foolishly missed that initial chance, then it was always a knockdown fight even to get agreement on the facts.

If the reports are good, yet things are not going well in an organization, you need to go look yourself. Don't expect always to be alerted by shifty-eyed reporters. Some untrustworthy eyes are the purest of steady blue. Don't expect slumped shoulders. Some people simply and truly believe all their own lies. Good luck in dealing with them. I have always had trouble.

There is another classic form of dishonesty you will occasionally meet. I think of it as the weakest shepherd case.

What usually happens is that you or one of your subordinates discovers that someone has unexpectedly forged or altered or made up a required record or report.

Sometimes what is there on the face of it is all there is. Some weak person failed to do what he should have and, when faced with a requirement he couldn't meet, he forged or altered or made it up.

However, sometimes there is more to it. How and why did the organization recruit such a weak person to fill a job that had that level of responsibility? How did he get through your training pipeline? Why didn't his supervisors realize that he was overloaded? Why is there such pressure on the person that it overcame his natural tendency to be honest? Who is exerting that pressure? Is the strain necessary or even desirable? Why didn't anyone help that individual?

By the time a senior supervisor is involved the individual has often been damaged beyond repair for his current environment. His dishonesty may well be the way he has chosen out of the situation he finds himself in—not everyone uses a knife to commit suicide.

I treat this type of dishonesty as a shepherd with a staff waving to say, "Look over here."

It is well worth a minute or two out of your busy day to look around the portion of the organization thus flagged. Perhaps there is no problem. However, this is an invitation to look that you would be foolish to ignore. Given the strength of the urge to be honest, think how strong the pressure must have been to force the violation of integrity.

The last time I ignored that flag, we failed to prevent a second officer in that same organization from committing suicide.

Let's go back to positive examples. Truth not only makes it easier to sleep at night, as the supply officer in one of the earlier examples failed to understand, but also makes it easier to answer questions later about past behavior. Personal integrity, and the enhanced reputation that inevitably results, is downright invaluable when the jobs get truly difficult.

Once upon a time, an officer was assigned a tough recovery job. The people assigning him knew it was going to be difficult. But, as usual in these cases, no one recognized how rotten the area had gotten. (An organization always underestimates the severity of a bad situation. If it had recognized the problem, it would have done something earlier.)

So, as various unexpected things came to light over the next year the assigned troubleshooter was blamed for some of them. In fact, formal court-martial charges were preferred against him three times during that year. This was not all bad. If losing isn't a possibility, where is the challenge that makes a job tough? If the job isn't tough, who wants it? At the same time, if you are continually having to check your footprints it is difficult to look ahead.

In tough jobs, you can't be worrying about what somebody is going to decide later should have been done. The best defense is to call it exactly as you see it and let the guys on the ground sort it out later. You can always call on Teddy Roosevelt to testify for your side. He wows them with that man-in-the-arena quote.* Whatever you do, don't look back. Let anyone investigate anything he wants, as long as he doesn't get in the way of progress.

By the way, none of the court-martial charges stuck. The third time the charges were dismissed, the organization also dismissed the officer who was writing the charges instead of helping.

Once upon a time we were playing at controlling submarines in a war game. Submarines are wonderful weapons. Because they are stealthy they can do lots of things. In wartime everybody wants one. If you are controlling them everyone is your friend. It's like being a kid and owning the only real baseball in your neighborhood.

We were sending submarines over here to identify these ships, and over there to land some clandestine agents, and down there to snoop around, and up someplace else to send a signal. We were having a hell of a good time. Then, all of a sudden, one of the umpires who was running the game came up to me and whispered that we had just lost one of our game submarines.

"What?"

"Yup. Ran him into your own mine field." He smirked the way guys do when you have just done something stupid. Pure jealousy. From

---

* "It is not the critic who counts, not the one who points out how the strong man stumbled, or where the doer of deeds might have done them better. The credit belongs to the man who is actually in the arena; whose face is marred with sweat and dust and blood; who strives valiantly; who errs and comes short again and again; who knows the great enthusiasms, the great devotions, and spends himself in a worthy cause; who at the best knows in the end the triumph of high achievement; and who at the worst, if he fails, at least fails while daring greatly, so that his place shall never be with those cold and timid souls who know neither victory nor defeat." *The American Treasury 1455-1955,* ed. Clifton Fadiman (New York: Harper & Brothers, 1955), 689.

his face you could see that he wished he had a baseball of his own. Probably didn't even own a glove.

The game went on for three more days. We sank hundreds of thousands of tons of warships. We lost other submarines to enemy action and other events. The staffs had a great time. The one early casualty became lost in the grass.

When you get done with a major exercise, the players usually pick what they want to report. The game is essentially for the education and edification of the players, and the players are usually more senior and understand better than any observer what is important. If you haven't ever been in a sophisticated war game it sounds funny; but because a war game is so complex and any game is only one very limited scenario of a very large set, reporting on yourself in a war game is not a bad system.

Of course, that gives the player some latitude in what he thinks is important enough to report. Often, the fact that you especially screwed up one particular aspect may not make the final cut in your report to your boss.

But a war game is most often an exercise for the staffs in how to shuffle the right paper to get the orders to forces to relocate, or to arrange for transportation to move weapons from here to there. Sometimes it is an exercise in grand strategy. Usually not. The losses and gains on the board or in the computer are a product of artificial rules. They bear little or no resemblance to what will happen when the fog of war settles down between the combatants at sea and the grand strategy makers ashore.

On the other hand, if the staff can't even control where it lays its own minefields, what help is it to the poor sons of bitches at sea?

So we said, in our report to our boss, that the highlight of the game from our aspect was that we had set up a situation that had sunk our own submarine, and that we would take corrective action and get back to him.

As reports go, our less-than-positive one was in the distinct minority.

We worked the problem. We dropped the priority on other projects. We redefined jobs and established special task forces with the redistributed manpower. We researched and thought. We travelled and investigated. We worked the problem for six months. Halfway through, we discovered that the problem was much worse than we had expected.

In fact, many of the mining plans in one part of the world were completely bollixed up. There wasn't one problem, there were about sixteen separate ones. No problem by itself was catastrophic, but when they were laid out on top of each other there was hardly one area in that part of the world that would have been safe to traverse by ship or scow. In the end, we found a reasonable solution that was quickly implemented.

If we had swept the problem under the rug no one would have been wiser. If we had swept the problem under the rug we would never have had to make the major effort that was finally required to fix it. However, we could not sweep the problem under the rug once we had decided to report it as a major problem. Reporting it meant we had to do something. It was a case of integrity acting as a forcing function for improvements.

Before we leave the subject of integrity, it is worthwhile to discuss it in the context of Washington duty. There are two primary battlegrounds in Washington: the Pentagon and the Congress.

In both truth gets you by when nothing else will.

In both there are a lot of people with a lot of personal agendas.

In the Pentagon and Congress there are a great number of jobs for which you may not feel prepared. Nobody is actually a professional at doing many of them. For instance, you may be asked to determine the answer to a problem that might occur sometime in the future if the world changes somewhat. You venture into the issue blindly and find three people inside the Beltway, all who have worked that exact problem for forty years. One solution seems reasonable but is very expensive, one solution seems cheap but violates two laws of physics, and the third guy seems just plain crazy. The last fellow is married to the chief of staff's oldest sister. On the Hill the relationships are even more Byzantine.

There is no right answer for any question tough enough to become a political question. You have to make decisions on what you believe is best for the nation. Integrity talks in Washington when all other decision guides are useless.

The most effective executive I ever worked for in Washington wore his integrity on his sleeve. He was a face-value person. He meant what he said, and he said what he meant. He made Horton, the elephant in the Dr. Seuss books, look like a piker.

He got tremendous results.

As a footnote for military officers who may be reading this: remember, whenever you are dealing with Congress, the other guys are the professional politicians. You are the professional warrior. The only thing you have to sell in Washington is your integrity. One rip in that fabric and you are a tailor without a product.

Integrity forces you to sail the right reach, helps you identify an acceptable course, provides the armor to battle the tough jobs, and by its absence warns of unexpected hazards. It even sells in the marbled and granite halls of Washington. Not a bad shipmate.

# CHAPTER SEVENTEEN

## Location

I t is difficult to be a leader if you are afraid. Troops quickly drop out from the ranks behind men who demonstrate an overly conspicuous concern for their own safety.

Good instinct. Men worrying about themselves generally don't have a lot of time left to spend thinking about others.

Yet, if the truth be known, most of us are afraid. We may not be afraid of mice, or worms, or spiders (small ones), but we all have fears. We were afraid even before we left our teens behind and were briefed on the secret that we are mortal.

Fortunately, bravery is a learned skill.

I once watched Admiral Rickover on the initial sea trials of a new submarine. (As I've said, he rode each and every one.) We made our first dive. On the way to test depth, the after escape trunk began leaking. Water was spraying into the small enclosed chamber from which we would have to escape if the submarine went down. We immediately surfaced and talked about what we should do.

It surely was a problem. The leak was inside the trunk, but with the ship on the surface there wasn't enough pressure to cause visible leakage. We thus couldn't see the problem unless we submerged again. Someone would have to get in the trunk to fix it, closing the hatch behind him. The hatch to the escape trunk opened into the trunk. If the submarine submerged and the leak got larger than the drain line would handle, the person in the trunk was going to be in the deep weeds. Once water was in the trunk the hatch could not be opened. It would be like trying to push open a door against a leaning elephant.

A half hour went by. Everyone stood around.

Suddenly Admiral Rickover's voice came over the speaker from the escape trunk, "Tell the conn to take this ship down to test depth. The engineer officer and I are in here, and we'll fix whatever leaks."

So we did. And they did.

The sea trials did not drag. We got back on schedule. Every event was accomplished successfully. Another fine ship delivered to the nation. No stories about a bad-luck ship, or questions about whether the submarine had been built too quickly. Just another little problem solved. We continued training. Admiral Rickover went back to Washington, D.C., and his uncarpeted little office.

None of us recognized it as bravery at the time. Once you think about it, all that could happen would be that the escape trunk would fill up and pressurize the men inside. A small air bubble would remain near the top. Which is exactly what would happen if you deliberately used the trunk for an escape. Worst thing that could happen to the people inside would be their eardrums might get broken. Maybe a little bends.

Heck, that was a good engineering decision that Rickover made. Getting into the trunk himself was the right thing. Would have done it myself if I had thought of it. Not really bravery.

I would follow that man, though.

Several years later, aboard another ship, we were having problems with the largest electrical motor aboard—a motor a little taller than the average man, and as big around as four kegs of beer. Not your average motor, surely, this one was too big to be removed easily from the ship. When it had been installed, the motor had been carefully insulated with coats of shellac to protect it against any and all moisture in the air. It had also been specially and completely encased in steel to prevent any water spray from reaching it, as well as to protect the fragile windings from somebody's careless wrench. Only then had the motor been placed aboard ship.

We, of course, had somehow gotten water inside it.

The choices were simple. We could uncouple the motor from its pump, remove the interfering piping, remove the couple of other pieces of equipment that were in the way, cut out the metal decking, and take the motor off the ship to be disassembled. It would be two days to maneuver it off the ship, five days for repairs ashore, and three days to rig the motor back aboard and reassemble it. That was choice number one.

Behind door number two was the option of starting the motor up and hoping that the heat of the electricity running gently through the windings would be enough to evaporate the water inside so as to permit the moisture to be carried off in the motor's normal cooling air flow. If it worked, we estimated the whole process would take about an hour. We had done the same thing before with a couple of smaller motors (each about the size of a large rabbit).

The ship was scheduled to get under way tomorrow.

We recognized that the downside of option number two was that if it didn't work we would have created conditions (water, metal, electricity) conducive to starting an electrical fire. Therefore we stationed some people with fire extinguishers, and established communications with the electrical switchboard so that we could quickly deenergize the motor if things went wrong. To be even more careful, I went out and positioned myself right next to the motor so I would quickly be able to smell any melting or burning shellac (byproducts of insulation deterioration).

"Start the motor," I said.

"Start the motor, aye, aye."

The electrician turned the switch and the electrical controller applied starting current (about the same amount used to supply a block of houses for a year). The current instantly vaporized the water in the motor. The water turned to steam. The steam expanded, pushing the coils in the motor closer together. The motor insulation cracked.

The fireball, about the size of a small pony, missed my face by a few inches, smashed against the switchboard, and ricocheted around the space, scaring the hell out of everybody and starting several small fires.

The only smell I caught was the stench of scorched eyebrows. Mine.

Door number two was not a good engineering decision.

If you do not understand something fully, and are going to take chances, it is best to put your own body up front. First of all, you tend to stop dangerous things sooner the closer your body is to the action end of the order chain. Which at least is one move in the right direction. Secondly, you don't hurt anyone you shouldn't. Third, if you are lucky and survive, the fact you did it yourself tends to cause the troops to gloss over how stupid it was in the first place.

\*    \*    \*

Once we were in overhaul in a shipyard that wanted to get out of the nuclear submarine overhaul business. As I may have mentioned previously, during a submarine overhaul the shipyard takes nearly everything out of the ship, refurbishes or replaces it, and then shoehorns it all back in. This shipyard's management was so anxious to stop submarine work that they appeared almost eager to demonstrate that they were too incompetent to perform. For starters they had taken nearly every one of their experienced workers out of the submarine overhaul business and put them on other, less demanding, and financially more rewarding work.

You may also recall from previous chapters that there are some submarine overhaul jobs that can only be tested at sea. The ship dives in water that is relatively shallow and tests some jobs, then moves over to deeper water to test the rest. It is a tense time. It can be particularly tense if you don't have any confidence in the people who have done the work.

In some situations, and this was one, there is nothing to do but push your way through by brute force. For over two years we had done our best to supervise the shipyard's work. Now we needed to put the ship through her paces. If we were careful, we would find everything the shipyard had screwed up before the mistakes killed us.

So we went to sea. We left the pier, maneuvered out the channel, submerged the ship, and started carefully running the ship through her paces.

The commanding officer went to sleep. Must have been tired. He slept for two days. He woke as we successfully completed the last dangerous evolution.

The commanding officer was a very bright, pleasant man. In fact, he was one of the most positive people I have known. Unfortunately, he did not have a good command tour. His ship always had more than its fair share of problems. There seemed to be no good reason for it, but people were always doing, or failing to do, the damnedest things aboard that submarine.

I am particularly interested in the events surrounding submarine groundings (hitting the bottom or shore), collisions (with ships, buoys, cables, etc.) and other serious mishaps over the last twenty-five years. Submarine mystery stories are one of the few things in this world that are both interesting and educational. Each investigation or mystery contains the same elements as the civilian genre (betrayal, heartbreak, mysterious strangers, etc.), combined with the foreboding certain knowledge that something horrid is about to happen.

The submarine service is a small organization. One inevitably meets and talks over coffee with men who were present, or who know parts that fit into the story. Some are bits that may have been considered peripheral at the time of the investigation. Sometimes happenings don't make complete sense until you actually meet the personalities involved.

However it occurs, the passage of time makes some events much clearer—the careful rubbing of old tombstones often uncovers interesting patterns. One is that the commanding officer was nearly always at the scene when an accident occurred and the executive officer was not. The first part of that seems logical. It is difficult for a serious accident to happen without the commanding officer personally exercising poor judgment. But what about the executive officer? He doesn't stand watches. He has many other duties, but his primary one is to back up the commanding officer. Where was he?

Depends on what happened.

If the casualty was that the submarine ran into a ship, then the executive officer was usually in the lower level engine room looking for dirt in the bilges. On the other hand, if there was a fire in the engineering spaces, the executive officer was usually up forward working on some paper project. Funny.

There are three possible explanations of the location of the mysteriously elusive executive officer. One: perhaps the executive officer is so critical to most ships' safe operation that submarines get in trouble anytime he isn't there.

Two: the pattern may just be due to chance.

Three: possibly some weak executive officers sense that a problem is developing and hide where they won't be involved. Possibly some weaker commanding officers are more comfortable without near-peers always looking over their shoulders and providing advice—and thus let their executive officers hide.

Who knows?

Years ago we were having a lot of problems during the very short periods the submarines were on the surface maneuvering into and out of ports. We were running into ships, buoys, rocks, logs; you name it—we hit it. When the accident happened the commanding officer was usually on the bridge; that's where he is supposed to be. Sometimes he was overwhelmed by the situation, or said "*left*" when he meant "*right*," or something. Whatever was happening, we were having lots of problems.

We made a rule that the executive officer had to be in Control (or topside on the deck), physically backing up the commanding officer, while entering and leaving every port.

Most good executive officers had been in Control, or taken station topside, before we made the rule. Now they all were.

Submarines stopped hitting things. Interesting.

I said bravery was a learned art. I meant it.

Everyone starts life afraid. It's not only natural, it isn't even a bad system. When danger becomes evident, some fear stimuli get the adrenaline pumping to provide quick fuel and other fear stimuli get the feet oriented in the right direction—away.

The problem is, if you are going to choose leadership as a profession you are going to have to overcome fear. Fear is a constant in a leader's environment. If you didn't have a fearful situation, why would an organization want a leader— just to establish head-of-the-line privileges for meals and the wooing of the other sex?

Nope, an organization only needs and will only support a leader when there is danger. The danger the organization faces may be the loss of market share or jobs; it may be the danger of not putting national resources where they are needed. Aboard a submarine, the danger is that you have to slay the dragon every time.

There is no place to run from danger aboard a submarine. Whether the dragon materializes in the form of fire, flooding, heat, loss of power, or something else, if you don't get the dragon the dragon eats you. The facts are simple. If you are in the leadership business, you cannot run away. You have to be in the business of not letting your body react naturally to fear.

The situation is similar to breaking a horse to saddle. The horse's natural inclination is to buck. That inclination has saved the horse's ancestors from mountain lions for thousands of years. But when they are saddled every day most horses learn to control their bucking instinct.

Because the leader knows that overcoming fear is part of his own job description, he should take each day and every opportunity to rein his mind and body into accommodating fear. The good leader thinks about as many dangerous situations as he can imagine, the possible alternatives, and what he should do. How long can he stay there before running? What are the alternatives? What are the consequences of losing control?

Thinking about all the physical, moral, and bureaucratic consequences usually makes one much better able to tolerate fear.

The good leader then seizes every opportunity to put himself where the danger is most intense.

Once upon a time aboard a submarine, a fire was reported in the torpedo room, where all of the high explosives were stowed. There were nine officers in the wardroom at the time of the first announcement. As you exited the wardroom the space with the fire was nine feet to the right. The space from which you took reports and coordinated efforts was forty feet to the left. The first seven officers out of the wardroom, as well as the ninth, turned left. They were going to do something that kept their hands clean. The eighth officer turned right, entered the problem compartment, and closed the watertight door to contain the flames. Either you slay the dragon. . . .

Someone who aspires to leadership has the choice of turning left to help "manage" a fire, or turning right and becoming part of the life-and-death struggle with the dragon. If he can control his feet, the leader always turns right. Otherwise, how do you ever know for sure that you have learned enough about fire fighting?

If the leader can't control his feet the first time, he thinks about it and either drops out of the leader business or practices some more until turning right becomes second nature.

The leader always fires the guns himself, at least once. He always handles the acids himself, at least once. He always pours the molten iron himself, at least once.

The aspiring leader puts his body where the danger is and lets his mind and body experience fear in all its forms. The man who will be a good leader learns through experience how close he can stand to the dragon's flame and still control those emotions.

It is all in where you place your body. In leadership, it's just as the real estate lady says, there are only three things that are important: location, location, and location.

# CHAPTER EIGHTEEN

## Communicating

C hoosing what and how juniors routinely report to their seniors is an important leadership decision.

For the boss, communications serve several business purposes as well as basic human needs. The most basic purpose of reports is to ensure that the supervisor is not surprised by something a subordinate does or experiences. If a boss is surprised, he suspects his subordinates were also surprised. There are no good surprises. A leader's job is to anticipate. If a subordinate appears not to be able to do so, it should not be a great surprise to him if his boss starts evaluating the need for a change.

Secondly, if you have a truly unusual and tough problem on the horizon, you need to give your boss time to think about it. When it is feasible, you should allot some time for your staff to work the problem, as well as setting aside some time for your own judgment to work. You should provide the same courtesies to your senior and his staff.

If your boss is rushed into making a bad decision, he may later forget the decision. He will never forget he was rushed.

Finally, no (or at least no to the nearest decimal point) leader has complete confidence in your loyalty to him and the organization. Yet, for him to sleep at night your supervisor needs to believe that you are working for the greater good of the organization (which inevitably becomes entangled or identical with the supervisor's image of his own best interests).

The junior must always ensure that his immediate supervisor is absolutely certain of the junior's personal loyalty. A new boss or an unself-confident one can make this difficult. Some job conditions can also make it hard to establish a trusting relationship—the more prestigious or powerful the junior's job, the more physically remote from the boss the junior's office, or the larger the junior's own personal constituency, the harder the junior must work to gain his senior's trust.

The situation may not demand kowtowing, but there are bureaucratic equivalents that are expected. It may be as simple as personally meeting your boss at the airport. It definitely includes telling your boss before you talk to someone senior to him in the organization or someone outside the organization. It always includes reports back to the senior of what went on.

Back to periodic routine reports. Once you have decided that you need to report something periodically the question becomes, "What's the period?" The short answer is, "About weekly."

A daily report, depending on the organization, is usually too frequent for busy people with full calendars. It's a lot, even if in your organization you are the straw that stirs the drink. Unless the unit has established a daily meeting to handle operational matters, weekly seems about right. A weekly review of what you have done, what you have learned, what is planned, and how those things have helped, will help, or will affect your boss, is about the right frequency and emphasis.

The ideal organization does not deliberately have one individual reporting to more than one boss. However, sometimes a leader will find himself in such a situation. While this is never an easy position, one principle to follow is not to make the same reports to any two people. You need to keep each advised, but advised about different aspects of your job, so there is less opportunity for one to make a decision about something that falls in the other's area of responsibility. Working for multiple bosses is a tough job. Good luck.

We have had some royal donnybrooks in the submarine force over who made what reports. In this as in so many other submarine issues, Admiral Rickover was instrumental in what was changed. Interestingly enough, when I look back, this was not so much a result of Admiral Rickover's personal leadership style (as many of us thought at the time) as of the bureaucratic "free market" process.

To understand what happened, you must realize that while the United States Congress and a few other foresighted leaders were building nuclear submarines and forcing them on the Navy, we (the Navy) kept the same infrastructure that had been in use when diesel submarines were not much more than fleet scouts. Nothing changed organizationally for a long time, despite the significant and eventually overwhelming differences in capability between a diesel and a nuclear platform.

Thus, for at least two decades after nuclear submarines started going to sea the supervisory structure above the submarine commanding officer level contained very few men who understood the material requirements or different operational capabilities of these nuclear submarines. In fact, many of the men serving as the immediate supervisors of nuclear submarine commanding officers were the same men Admiral Rickover had passed by as candidates for service in these new nuclear-powered submarines.

Yes, your instincts are correct, there were some tensions.

As late as 1970, sixteen years after the *Nautilus*'s first underway, neither the engineer nor the division commanders in the *Nautilus*'s squadron (the immediate supervisory group responsible for the maintenance and training of six to twelve submarines) were nuclear trained, much less nuclear experienced.* Several of the supervisors were in fact openly hostile to providing the most elementary assistance (their primary job) to nuclear submarines.

On the other hand, on his staff (often called "Naval Reactors") in Washington, D.C., Admiral Rickover had assembled a group of men who understood submarine design and material problems** and were

---

* Going through the twelve-month nuclear training pipeline (six months classroom theory, six months practical experience on an operating reactor) did not make you a nuclear-experienced officer. It was not until most men had worked for several years in the fleet with the system that Admiral Rickover had established that they began to understand the need for such rigid standards, neverending training, and close supervision. Until you understood, you were not an effective nuclear supervisor.

** The men on his staff were and had been personally involved in the design of the submarines' nuclear engineering plants. If the person you called had not had a hand in deciding the size or the shape of a particular device in which you were interested, the person at the next desk had. Once I called Naval Reactors with a question and the third senior person there was called to the telephone, listened to my problem, and then asked me to go back under the deckplate in the Top Hat area and see if the unmarked switch mounted on the I-beam was in the forward or aft position. I looked. It was forward. He then carefully explained to me what the switch did and why it had to be in the aft position. Support like that made it easy to appreciate that everyone was working toward a common goal.

tasked by him with supporting the fleet. Instead of officers on a submarine calling D.C. and being connected with a phone that was never answered, reaching an office in which a decision was never made, or getting the runaround when they needed help to get a running start, results that had been all too common, they received an immediate answer or a quick call-back when they called Naval Reactors. If you were an engineer or a commanding officer of a submarine in the fifties, sixties, and early seventies, you could always get a better answer faster if you personally called Naval Reactors direct. You received little or no help from the two organizational layers between the ship and Naval Reactors.

It was an interesting process to observe. It was not that people were deliberately flouting the chain of command, it was that because Rickover offered the marketplace (the submarines) a much better product, he practically cornered the market. On the other hand, because the chain of command process provided very little added value, the submarine chain of command received only lip service.

During this period we wanted to make some changes in the way we operated on the ship I served on. In fact, for several reasons it had been a couple of years since adequate attention had been paid to the procedures used to operate the ship. In that time, much of the ship's equipment had been changed. It was now virtually impossible to operate this particular submarine properly with the existing procedures.

We carefully wrote up new, corrected procedures and submitted them to the squadron (our submarine's immediate supervisor), and the squadron passed our letters on to the type commander (the next level up) for approval. We submitted letters for more than a year. No reply. No reply to our phone calls requesting status. Nothing. Finally, we asked Admiral Rickover for help. When his staff got involved they found 136 unanswered and unstaffed letters* in the type commander's office from our ship alone.

The type commander's staff members were not qualified to judge whether the letters were even roughly right, much less whether the

---

* It has been twenty years. I can still remember how mad and frustrated I was at the time to find that nothing had been done with our months of effort. By the way, 136 is an exact number.

recommendations were safe. So they had sat on them, apparently to emphasize their own importance in the chain of command. Within a month after Naval Reactors got involved all of the letters and most of the issues had been resolved.

One of the hot topics of the sixties and seventies was the debate on whether Admiral Rickover and his unorthodox personal and engineering reporting requirements were destroying the chain of command. When I look around the submarine force nearly twenty years later, none of the requirements has changed, but there no longer is a controversy. What has happened in the interim is that the squadron and type commander staffs have acquired technical and administrative competence. Today, Naval Reactors no longer has the same market share. They always had some inherent disadvantages in a free market. Once their product was only about twice as good as what the squadrons' and type commanders' staffs could provide, Naval Reactors lost most of their customers.

The value of the chain of command was easily visible once the chain of command started adding value.

Let's look at an example of that value. If you were a ship's engineer with a problem and called Admiral Rickover's office to talk to one of the staff, and if that staff member happened to decide that your question or the ensuing discussion demonstrated a significant lack of understanding, or if you accidentally trod on the organizational hot button of the day (oh yes, Naval Reactors has them too), you might very well have ended up unexpectedly talking to one of his very senior staffers or to Admiral Rickover himself. If they or he did not like your answers, in addition to making you feel stupid (which was bad enough for your ego), he might pass his displeasure down the chain.

That is a hell of a downside for one direct-dial telephone call.

On the other hand, if you could walk into the office of your immediate boss, whom you knew a great deal better than you did Admiral Rickover, and sit down over a cup of coffee to pose your problem, and get your boss to either answer your question, discuss what the limits of the options were, or carry the question forward himself—then if Admiral Rickover thought the question was stupid you weren't going to be the one who got called names.

From the bottom looking up, advice, counsel, and protection from the wrath of the higher-ups is the major bureaucratic advantage of the chain of command. The chain of command has to be terribly incompetent or ineffective for the average leader to forsake its cover.

There is a general lesson here. If people are bypassing the established chain of command, it should be clear evidence that the situation is bollixed. The consumer has decided that the chain provides no added value. There are always significant disadvantages in bypassing the chain of command. Only a fool or a fanatic would do so—if there were any other option.

In addition to insisting that each submarine had the right to call his office for technical advice (a right used advisedly, and, as pointed out, a right that had less value and was exercised much less frequently as the senior staffs became progressively more able to deal with nuclear engineering support questions), Admiral Rickover insisted that each submarine commanding officer write him personal letters. The required frequency of the letters depended upon how much engineering work you were doing. If the ship was in the portion of the operating cycle when it was never in the shipyard, the frequency was three months; if the ship was in a shipyard overhaul, the frequency was every two weeks.

Some people hated the letters (and still do). Admiral Rickover wanted a summary of what the ship had been doing and what engineering problems you were having.

My best guess is that he started the letters because he was looking for inputs on operational nuclear submarine achievements. The diesel-dominated submarine chain of command was not terribly interested in talking all the time about all the things that nuclear submarines could do before breakfast that diesel boats could not accomplish in a month of Sundays (there were obviously farsighted men who were exceptions). However, it was exactly those "firsts" and other unique achievements that Admiral Rickover was using to encourage Congress to build the nuclear submarine fleet.

Recall the times. Do you remember that sending the *Nautilus* under the North Pole was the first American reply to *Sputnik?*

If you read any of Admiral Rickover's congressional testimony during the fifties and sixties, you will find it replete with comments on the significant operational accomplishments of nuclear submarines. It was very effective politicking (in addition to being militarily correct). At the same time, many of the diesel boat heroes from World

War II must have felt that their blood-drenched heritage was being ripped from them by some ill-qualified officer who hadn't even had a submarine command. Many senior Navy submariners were not interested in helping Admiral Rickover.

Concurrently, across the river from Congress in the Pentagon, the submarine force was organizationally subordinate to the surface ship community. In fact, it was the surface ship construction budget that was being used to fund these new submarines, especially the Polaris missile ones. Nuclear submarines were being built out of the very hide of the surface ship force structure.

At the same time, it quickly became obvious that a nuclear submarine could go faster, turn more quickly, and stay at sea longer than a surface ship. It was, in fact, the first true stealth platform, and it was going to make antisubmarine warfare for the surface ship community even more difficult.

As neither the senior submarine community nor the Pentagon was interested in telling Admiral Rickover how well the nuclear submarines were doing at sea, he asked the submarine commanding officers to tell him. They were more than happy to do so. Nothing like being asked to tell somebody how well you are doing.

Over the years, the letters to Rickover changed as the submarine force changed. Nuclear-trained submariners started filling the key billets in the submarine force chain of command. In the Pentagon, submarines were divorced from the surface ship directorate and given their own slice of responsibility. Concurrently, Admiral Rickover began to limit his interest to the engineering-related problems ships were experiencing.*

Some people never had a problem with the letters. Instead of waiting until the day before the letter was due to sit down and begin writing blindly, they built their letters every week, using the requirement as

---

* With the caveat that if one area became fouled up beyond belief, he might define it (temporarily or permanently) as being within his area of responsibility, as it affected the nuclear propulsion plant or its people. A good example was atmosphere control. We had not managed to develop a good system of reliable equipment or reliable monitoring. He recognized the importance of this area and took it over until the problems were solved.

an opportunity to sit down and reflect on what had happened aboard their ship that week, what events seemed to mean or portend, and what the thoughtful leader would do. What was the big picture?

It was always surprising to me how useful this weekly moment was. Sometimes we are so busy and rushed that without external prompting it is easy to make decisions minute to minute or day to day, and get so caught up in working hard that we do not stop to question if these decisions we have made, when taken all together, make a lot of sense.

Other times, one has blithely walked under and amongst so many trees that one has no idea they have become a forest. It is only when the individual sits down and tries to contemplate what is happening that he becomes aware that the sun has dipped below the horizon and he has been tripping over tree roots for an hour. Maybe the right answer is to camp for the night. Maybe the right answer is to get out of the woods. Maybe he only has to take out his flashlight. Whatever the answer, stopping to realize what is going on has prevented many a bad fall.

I like the idea of a periodic written self-review. When I was in command, we started writing a "Rickover letter" on the nonengineering portion of the ship. We wrote it just for ourselves for a year. We were interested in finding out whether it was useful because it stimulated thought and self-evaluation, or whether we were doing it for engineering only because Admiral Rickover demanded it.

Turns out that many ideas that sound good in conversation, or "think good" in your mind, do not meet the black-and-white sanity check of pencil on paper. Periodic self-review is in itself a useful process. After a trial year we established periodic self-review reports as a routine.

There are a couple of special reports that are worth discussing. One is a nonperiodic, routine report in which you establish accountability for something or other. For example, in the Navy, when we change who is in charge of an organization or one of its units the person who is taking over submits a letter report. Many times there is something seriously wrong, but he fails to report it. Sometimes the new guy doesn't realize it is wrong. On the other hand, sometimes the new guy doesn't want to rock the boat, or offend anyone.

When problems break like a Midwestern thundercloud later, drenching all in the area, it is difficult to say that you knew it was coming all along when there is a document lying around with your signature on it that says you didn't recognize there was anything wrong. At least you didn't at the beginning. Maybe there wasn't anything wrong then. Maybe it is all your fault.

If there is something seriously wrong and you don't immediately identify it to your boss, you may have, with your first step aboard, quickly become part of the problem instead of the solution. The first shot is an opportunity that should not be wasted. Think about it this way: what do you not wish to be held accountable for? If there is nothing, no sweat. Those should be the usual circumstances.

If there is something, why not report it? Not being a snitch went out in high school. All that usually happens is that you will be told to fix it, which you were going to do anyway. Should you carry the worry of recognizing something is grossly wrong and yet not knowing if anyone else knows? Is your new boss going to think you are reliable if you knew something was wrong and didn't tell him?

The second special report is also one that reports something is wrong. It is the one you write to put on the record that a situation exists when it is so bad that the organization should not permit it to continue to exist. I knew someone who decided his ship was in such poor material condition that it should be decommissioned well before its expected lifetime. He wrote a letter via the chain of command to the secretary of the Navy. His letter was disapproved.

Six months later an inspection team came aboard and said, "Whoa there, this ship is in dangerous material condition!"

And he said, "Yes, I know, I have officially so informed the chain of command." And produced his letter and all the endorsements thereto.

And he finally got some help.

That's the right place to end this chapter, with the good guys winning another one.

# CHAPTER NINETEEN

## Bullets

Everyone makes a mistake now and then. Some of the mistakes flash in our organizational consciousness and are gone just as quickly, like a shooting star on a summer night. Others seem no more powerful at first. Appearing as faint streaks of light, they blossom once, and again, ever higher, and again, like a fireworks extravaganza at the ball park on the Fourth of July. Sometimes a mistake sprays bullets and kills someone. What makes the difference? How does one person survive a mistake that is deadly to another?

Recovering from adversity requires an individual to demonstrate that he understands what happened, recognizes why the event was serious, and has undertaken the changes necessary to correct the problem. These are all steps an individual takes to recover from a mistake.

On the other hand, whatever happened may well prove to be an error from which you cannot possibly recover. There are limits in every business to what is acceptable.

But if you have swung beyond those limits, that should not affect your recovery efforts. Worrying over spilt milk is as worthless as the nursery story implies. Instead, work on what is within your control. Follow the same recovery path you would if the incident were survivable. Remember that your boss may well have come close to a similar incident, or have been involved in one himself. He probably has seen many worse errors. What do you think he is watching for now?

Your boss is interested in whether the error was due to a momentary misjudgment that should be laid at the feet of the god of aggressiveness, or due to your judgment being seriously flawed with respect to basic aspects of the profession. He is looking for indications that will help him make a decision. One of the first things he looks at is whether you recognize what the error says about your entire organization.

If sufficient thought or care has gone into the design of the organizational system one error does not result in a major problem. Every system should have multiple safeguards (for example, design, rules, procedures, training, and personal judgment). One or two mistakes should not be enough to cause disaster. Most organizations have a multiple safeguard system that works day and night. For the thief to steal the jewels he must get over the river (and the drawbridge is raised), over the electric fence, past the guard dogs, past the electric eyes on the lawn, and through the locks on the doors and windows; and then he must find the combination to the safe in the bedroom floor.

Forgetting to put the dogs out when you leave will not result in the duchess losing her jewels. Not so long as you have remembered to raise the drawbridge and turn the fence on, cut the lawn, lock the doors and windows, put the rug back down, and chew up the combination to the safe.

The manor will be safer if you have also remembered the dogs, because someone living upstream from the castle could well have forgotten to tie up his boat. As a result, chance may send his punt drifting down the river and ashore near the thief.

But in all probability the duke and duchess could forget two or three of the independent safeguards and the jewels still would be safe. In fact, they probably do forget one or two of the checks each time the limousine leaves the grounds.

If you have had a serious accident, it is not only because your spouse forgot to kick the rug back over the safe in the bedroom.

Instead, it is because all of the safeguards have finally been disregarded simultaneously. Corrective action will need to address more than retraining your noble spouse. Everyone in the manor staff has failed to do something, and why, oh why, did not the duke or duchess note that things were deteriorating?

Your boss understands this principle. He is interested in seeing whether you are able to look beyond the immediate cause and identify the basic flaws. Do you recognize that the incident is a statement about your basic operating policies, or do you treat it as an isolated problem?

When you made a mistake in the nuclear submarine business, Admiral Rickover required you to write down what had happened, what you evaluated as the cause, and the corrective action you had taken. In addition to being a way to get quick feedback on items that needed to be re-designed or changed by senior commands, the system was an excellent device for determining whether the person in charge of the unit actually understood the basic cause of the error and was taking proper and adequate corrective action.

Just as with an essay (as contrasted with a true/false) quiz in school, when you have to write out your conclusions it is difficult to hide misunderstandings.

There was a format for writing these reports, and near the top of the report the author could ascribe the basic cause of the incident to one of five reasons. One could choose among:

1. Act of God
2. Design
3. Procedure
4. Personnel
5. Material

Woe be to the individual who put down "design" or "material" without actually knowing what he was talking about.* Double-woe to anyone who choose the top item in the list.

When something went wrong, if you approached the corrective action

---

* One very unlucky commanding officer had an incident in which an electrical breaker opened unexpectedly. He couldn't find anyone who would own up to opening the breaker, and no one could remember what the electrical panel meters had read (the easiest way to tell if the conditions for an automatic trip had been met). The culprit did not volunteer that he had done something stupid. Anyway, in this case, the com- manding officer chose to designate the cause as design. (For some incidents, you have to have more than a little detective blood in your lineage.)

Unfortunately (I said he was unlucky), Admiral Rickover had, in a previous job, personally designed that breaker, and so took it upon himself to explain in very clear terms, in a letter sent to the commanding officer (copies to the rest of the nuclear world) why design could not possibly be the answer.

It was like hitting that particular commanding officer with a baseball bat, but Ad- miral Rickover wanted to make a point. He did not want the designation of fault to be a casual decision. He wanted you to understand exactly what had happened and be able to stand behind your detective work.

from the aspect of wanting to root out the underlying causes to prevent it from happening again, it was usually easy to figure out what should be done. Sometimes it took some time, and often it took some effort, but all of the problems were eventually traceable to a series of mistakes. Most of the mistakes were personnel mistakes. A lesser number were related to procedures. Some were caused by the wrong material, or a bad design. There have been few, if any, that could be explained away only as acts of God.*

If you have a subordinate who believes his failures are due to acts of God, do you want to continue to employ him? Neither do I. Neither does your boss.

Your boss also does not want to have to coach you to recognize your mistakes. If you want to recover from an error, get out ahead of your boss in identifying what has to be done for corrective action. If you are out ahead, your boss will often choose to spend his time on something that more obviously needs his attention. If you are not, he cannot.

We have been discussing how to take an organizational hit, like a bullet right in the chest, and survive. Making a mistake is not the only potentially disastrous bullet that ricochets around an organization. There is also the bullet labeled "limited adaptability."

When you have taken a position, and your boss says that he doesn't think that position is correct or good or best, how do you handle that information?

One person with whom I worked always immediately rolled back into and tried to overrun his boss's objections. If he lost that appeal, then an hour or so later he would rethink his position and return to discuss it. The second time around, his rethought position was always sound. Unfortunately, it didn't often carry the day, because his first rebuttal had already forced his boss into a definite position.

It was interesting to observe his relations with his seniors. The junior individual had excellent judgment; but because he would always try first to overrun his boss's position, his bosses tended to disregard the

---

* Which is not to say people didn't try. It is to say that checking this particular block as the cause was a way to ensure you received a lot of senior help in finding the real factors.

first volley and not listen to the second (which occurred after the individual rethought his position).

This individual always poisoned the well during his initial trip.

It is difficult for anyone to get two drinks from the same bureaucratic well. The queue is usually too long. By the time you get back in line and shuffle forward for another audience, the questions and the situation have changed.

A second individual I watched apparently had the ability to rethink his position on the spot. He could take in his boss's input, instantly regroup, evaluate which aspect of his recommendation he held most dear, and reformulate it. He was impressive to watch. He won most of the discussions. If you can do it, flaunt it!

I have never been able to rethink my position immediately if my recommendation was overridden. I have always wanted a minute to think. If what I have recommended is not accepted, what is it that I don't know? To which factors is my boss assigning a different value? What have I missed? If I decide I haven't overlooked something important, I always take several moments to review whether I can live with his decision.

As I don't think as fast on the spot as many, unless the issue is one that has to be settled right now, especially when I find myself on the other end of the teeter-totter from my boss, I have made it a practice to roger for my senior's guidance and then think about it for a while. At least this course means he is not publicly in cement if I decide I need to revisit the issue. And if I really care, by choosing the time of rebuttal I can also choose the audience (usually just him), plus the package of accouterments with which I want to display the issue.

There are many equally good ways to deal with an adverse decision from your boss. The only bad way is to argue in front of others when you have been surprised and haven't planned, or can't adequately plan, in the time the air is going from your diaphragm up to your vocal chords, how you intend to present your argument.

If you are the boss, you should discuss your values with your subordinates early and often. The habit can prevent a lot of hot air and wasted time later.

How do you recover from a decision going against you? As a subtopic, how do you tell your boss no?

There is no way to gloss over the bureaucratic negatives of losing a major decision. Once you have been associated publicly with a particular position, losing even once affects your ability to get things done everywhere in the organization. The effects are not limited to the area you lost. Losing is not fun.

At the same time, it happens to the best of us now and then. Sometimes our boss may decide we lose, if only to remind us who is the boss. Occasional losses also ensure we don't suffer from ego oversufficiency, a potentially deadly organizational disease.

There are two approaches when you have lost. The first is to say, *"OK,"* and conduct a little private soul-searching to determine why it happened. There will be other days and other questions. The OK response is the response that is always preferred.

Unfortunately, sometimes your boss will make a decision that you find impossible to support. It is not that you are disloyal, but you do not believe in The Answer and will only do him a disservice to continue to work in that area.

In this case you may very well need to take the necessary steps to get out of the area, out of the task force, and formally transfer responsibility for the program. Do whatever is necessary so that when you are asked (and you will be) by the press or one of your supervisor's enemies, you can plead ignorance, or can truthfully say that you are the possessor only of old information on the subject. Then go out of the way to avoid the issue.

Whatever you do, never work against the decision, no matter how strongly you feel. You will inevitably be solicited, but any action is sure death.

Meanwhile, think of ways out for your boss, in the event you prove to have been right. Loyalty counts, even in defeat, and loyalty can be made compatible with integrity.

On to the interesting problem of successfully telling your boss no.

Although most people prefer consensus, and also want to use their subordinates as sounding boards for problems and decisions, a tentative decision or an opinion voiced by someone senior cannot be treated lightly by his staff or other juniors. A senior's subconscious evaluation should be almost right on the money at least eighty percent of the time. Remember, he got where he is by making good decisions.

Not only is he most probably right, it is always difficult for a boss, even one with supreme self-confidence, to hear "No, you don't understand," in public without causing his jaw to tighten at least slightly.

If it is at all possible, negative discussions are best held in private. However, sometimes that is impossible due to time constraints, schedule constraints, or the dynamics of the meeting. When disagreement has to be made in public, never treat it lightly, no matter what. Directing your boss to a better position always requires enormous concentration and energy. In public it is a hundred times harder.

There is no best way. One that is sometimes acceptable is to characterize to him the problems you would have in presenting his position and, at the same time, to introduce some new factors that will give him a public excuse to pause, such as the following:

"I would be reluctant to present that option today; the concept sounds good, but I wouldn't have a good backup answer if he (your supervisor's supervisor) asked what all the equal-cost alternatives were. If you can avoid getting into that subject today, my staff could run those alternatives out for you, and look at both kills per round as well as accuracy, for guns and pulsed weapons as well as missiles, and get them to you late tomorrow."

This is a silent plea along the lines of "I'm not sure, I think that you need to consider kills per round (a measure I may have just made up) as well as accuracy. I'm not sure you have considered the logical options to missiles. Give me a day to come up with some numbers (and a day to think about it; I have a funny feeling we're looking at the wrong measures of effectiveness)."

There were four parts to this quick answer to the boss's suggestion that he present this new option. First, although you think this is a great mistake (or you wouldn't even attempt to stop him), make a strong effort not to be negative early, no matter what. It is too easy to kill a fledgling idea. That is precisely what prevents needed change. You don't want to be guilty of negative vibes. At least nurture the new idea until you fully understand what it might become. Then, if you decide you truly need to kill it, it is best to blow the idea away in one blast. Much time has been wasted on dumb ideas that were only wounded the first time they flew and subsequently reappeared again and again, wandering about the bureaucratic underbrush.

Second, if it is at all feasible introduce something new into the equation that appears relevant, and that (you hope) your boss hasn't previously considered. Give your boss a reason not to act now.

Third, volunteer to be responsible for the work that is necessary for him to reconsider the idea.* This looks fair to everyone, and has the side benefit of giving you entree into the presentation and decision-making process.

Fourth, give your boss a definite time when you will report back. It needs to be obvious that you are not trying to outwait him on the issue, that you have voluntarily put your feet to the fire with an optimistic deadline.

You will probably still lose. However, you owe it to your boss to try. Nothing is easy. Telling your boss no in public is downright hard.

A good leader does not routinely operate at anywhere near his physical or emotional capacity. The good leader is always pacing his efforts so that he has enough reserve to sustain his concentration as long as necessary when unexpected events require.

It is possible to produce extraordinary professional efforts over a sustained period—years in some cases. Sometimes—war, for example, or the merger of your company, or when a family member is threatened—such an effort may be justified. However, the problem with operating at maximum capability is that the individual then cannot accept, or has difficulty accepting, emergent or emergency taskings. Not only will his interpersonal relationships suffer, he is not reliable, for he will stumble over the most elementary additional tasks and he will choose not to take on a job he should. Because that performance will be out of character, his boss will be unable to count on him.

A person operating near one hundred percent capacity is a person operating at the edge of his envelope of reliability.

He will not have the ability to take a bullet—of any caliber.

---

* Doing all the work is a good idea any time you want to convince someone. Whenever you want to get someone to change or establish something new, instead of just writing a convincing argument or brief, you should prepare all the paperwork (for all supervisory levels) necessary to put a positive decision on your idea into being. Writing all the paperwork makes you consider the problem from different views, and having to consider the implementation problems may cause you to repackage the idea in a more easily acceptable manner.

*     *     *

No individual is so good or so indispensable that he is immune to professional trauma. It's all in the leadership game. Susceptibility to taking a bullet is one of the downsides of the game. The ability to recover from adversity is an ability a leader must have. He is always going to need it.

The good leader has accumulated some extra professional goodwill for the eventuality. He also has already planned how he will execute his recovery. To one of life's grasshoppers, it will look like magic.

# CHAPTER TWENTY

## Opportunities

T ell them what you are going to tell them.
Okay.
Life is short. The moment is now. Never miss the chance to take a shower.
*Tell them.*
A leader needs experience. All experiences are useful. There is neither sufficient time nor a surfeit of opportunities.

Experience is the best teacher. Nothing is more helpful than experience in understanding the full range and impact of human emotions. This is particularly true with respect to learning how to deal with your own emotions. It is only with the aid of experience that a leader learns how to work through and outlast fear's paralyzing physical and mental manifestations.

Experience comes from undertaking challenges. Each challenge accepted, whether bested or not, becomes another experience recorded and filed for recall. I have an antique Korean medicine chest in my living room. This beautifully lacquered piece seems to have hundreds of individual little drawers. I visualize some old man using it to store countless medical herbs. My wife and I use the drawers for special keepsakes, such as an arrowhead, stubs from a Broadway show, a poem we both like, and so on. Each small box has become the storage vault for a special memory.

A leader is constantly looking for experiences to place in each drawer in his own medicine chest. A sidestepped challenge results in an empty drawer. A beautifully lacquered empty drawer, but an empty one nevertheless. One empty box that will never be filled by a victorious memory—because the challenge was avoided.

An opportunity, once turned away, can never be duplicated. The next challenge, like the next wave in the ocean, is not only different from its predecessor but will likewise be different from any swell that follows.

When I was in college I never made it over the wall on the obstacle course in full stride. I made it over, but never with the fluid motion that others demonstrated. I still remember struggling over that wall for the final trial my senior year and quitting with only a passing time. In my dreams, I have returned to that wall again and again. The remembrance of the acceleration until a yard and a half short of the base of the wall, the push-off that starts at the heel and goes through the straining arch onto the toe, the planting of my step into the wall, the bending of the knee, the pivot of the body into and then up, and the next step over—that drawer in my memory chest remains empty. My twenties were the time for that, if it was to happen. I turned away from that wall before I did it right. I do not know what use the experience would have been. I will never know.

Life is short. Challenges avoided are opportunities for experience that will never occur again. Men and women who would be prospective leaders must look for challenges.

After college a group of us underwent training to enter the Navy nuclear power field. Some of us were not engineering students, nor engineering oriented. We had completed college with relief, more than ready to abandon all campuses and get on with life. We had volunteered for nuclear submarines for the chance to be leaders in the country's newest and most exciting service branch. Maybe the extra money paid submariners also made a difference. Nevertheless, we had not volunteered for more time in a classroom.

We were now looking at another year of school. And it wasn't a liberal arts curriculum, in which you could get by with skimming a couple of books a week while lying under some tree, and writing two thousand words (four hundred original), accompanied by lots of copied footnotes. Solid B+ work.

No, we were now staring down the barrel of a complete engineering package. In fact, we were faced with a downright hard course. Eight hours of classroom time each day (only four hours on Saturday, and Sunday completely off), and another four to eight hours of study at home each night (four hours of which were required to be performed in the classroom for students with less than a C average).

Some of us sighed and buckled down, and learned about entropy and enthalpy, or at least learned that they were not alternate but equally acceptable spellings. We may not have understood everything, and to this day may not enjoy differential equations, but we accepted the curriculum as our first professional challenge. We still made it to San Francisco for the important things. We watched Willie Mays run and hit and catch, saw Carol Doda swing out over the crowd, and located the Purple Onion. Six months passed and the books were set aside to learn how to organize and supervise the people who turned the valves, operated the switches, and calculated the logarithms that made a nuclear reactor work. Pretty interesting, actually. Got to see Admiral Rickover once—from a distance—or somebody who looked a lot like him. Met my sweetie.

As it turned out, it wasn't such a bad time for some of us.

For others, it was the worst of times. Some did not like engineering, were not going to like it, and were determined not to find anything at all to enjoy about being young and tireless, and having the evenings and most of the weekends free within easy driving distance of San Francisco.

They were people who were unhappy with what they were doing. They studied only enough to get by and thus were not quite prepared for each higher level. They watched TV in their apartments until late and dozed during working hours. They resisted each new experience. They lasted the twelve months of schooling and the subsequent three or four years of obligated service and then left the Navy to restart their lives. They were very talented people. All of the ones I have kept in touch with are as successful as they wanted to be.

It is a shame they lost those four years. Too bad they avoided new experiences. Turns out that running one organization requires many of the same basic skills used in managing any other. The people you are going to work with are all the same. Turns out that trying to do something well, for which you do not have a strong aptitude, teaches interesting skills in concentration, perseverance, and brute-force-obstacle-overcoming (short title, you-would-be-surprised-at-the-problems-that-yield-to-uninformed-but-persistent-effort). Tough to lose four years.

Life is too short. It is a mistake to live entirely in the future. The future is much too uncertain. The moment is now.

Once upon a time a friend of mine wanted to attend graduate school. He wasn't sure what it would do for him, but it looked like something his peers were doing.

The course required two years attendance for the award of a master's degree. The school said they might be able to squeeze that down all the way to a minimum of eighteen months if he attended summer school.

His detailer (the man in Washington who actually told him where he had to go) said that he could attend school for only a maximum of twelve months and that failure to acquire a degree would reflect poorly on his record. His detailer strongly advised him to skip the school and go directly to another submarine job.

My friend wanted to go to school. What was the worst that would happen if he didn't graduate? His mother would still love him. He decided to enroll. He took some extra courses, putting in a few more hours each night. He used all his saved-up leave and vacation time to stretch the allotted year to thirteen months. He got the degree. All in all, he felt he learned a great deal. Says that it has been very useful since.

The moment is now.

Nearly every organization requires budding executives to move around to various parts of the country and perform different jobs. Sometimes one meets people who are terribly, or at least partially, unhappy in their current jobs, but are holding on because the next assignment they believe they are in line for will be terrific. That approach doesn't seem quite bright.

Who knows if you are going to get the next job? If there is not some risk in obtaining that job, then you are not in a very demanding line of work. On the other hand, if there is some risk, why give up being happy now in exchange for some imagined future good deal that may never take place?

An alternative is to change the current job so that you do enjoy it. Modify the job so it better fits your talents and interests. Do it your way. Don't worry about others perhaps not being pleased. If you have the talent to be a leader you can always find a job. Keep some "screw-you" money in your hip pocket and either enjoy the job, modify the job so you do enjoy it, or quit it and find something you do like. If you can't quit, then definitely change the job. It isn't practical to expect to perform a competent professional job doing a task in which you can't find personal satisfaction.

If you are not enjoying yourself, then how can anyone around you be having any fun? You can't work as hard as you should at something you don't enjoy. The moment is now. The future is exactly that.

Aboard a submarine at sea, surrounded by seawater, the biggest concern is having enough fresh water. The propulsion plant uses fresh water. The propulsion plant will not operate without it. People drink water. They also will not operate without it. The submarine can't do anything without power and people. All other fresh water uses are therefore accorded secondary priority.

When the submarine is at sea, every day is an opportunity that must be seized. Each day poses a challenge that must be met. There is training to be conducted that can be performed only at sea. Equipment is breaking and must be fixed immediately. There are evolutions to be performed, drills to be run, and exercises to do. Every action requires attention to detail, a great deal of effort, and some risk. There is tension, fear, and always the very real danger of dying.

At the end of the day nearly every man aboard a submarine is so tired he is gasping for sleep.

Most of the drills and evolutions routinely practiced require shutting down the machines that distill seawater into fresh water. Even if you were not so tired that all you wanted was sleep, often, at the end of the day, there is not even enough extra fresh water aboard the submarine for a shower.

On the other hand, if you do have sufficient fresh water to "waste" on a shower it is a good indication that everything is under control. The training went well. Unexpected glitches were solved. There were no real casualties today. There is enough water for the ship for the night and the morrow. You have lived through another twenty-four hours under the sea.

Life and death situations sometimes sneak up on one as quietly and unnoticed as a San Francisco fog. Correctly identifying an extreme situation is not a trivial task, only the initial one. Once safely over that first hurdle, the man who would seize glory must have sufficient physical reserve to lead the fight while concurrently, and coolly, evaluating progress. Despite one's hopes and good resolves, not every situation turns out for the best. A leader must have enough mental stamina to be able to see clearly through the gathering mist of fear and recognize when to cut his losses. Then, when he is ultimately successful, he must not neglect the opportunity to demonstrate to his troops how the fragrance of eventual success overpowers lesser odors.

Perhaps a final story will illustrate these points.

One summer our ship was operating near Bermuda. Nice place for vacations. Sunny. Nearly always clear weather. Good home port for the airplane crews who were testing out some tactics with us. Not a particularly fun place for a submarine to operate. Has nothing to do with the gorgeous jagged coral reefs. The reefs can be avoided. Has everything to do with that hot sun. Even at night it is impossible to get away from the heat. The summer seawater temperature around the island of Bermuda, as far down as several hundred feet, routinely runs in the high nineties. In a submarine high water temperatures result in a much higher air conditioning load. The air conditioning system is not only dealing with all the sweaty sailors and the heat from the engineering plant but also is laboring vainly to cool down part of the surrounding ocean.

We were on a voyage out of our home port in Connecticut, and had been struggling with our air conditioning system the entire trip. On this particular ship we had eight individual air conditioning plants powered by four different motors. If all of the plants were operating properly we had more than one hundred percent extra capacity. Unfortunately, over the twenty years the submarine had been in commission some of the insulation that normally contained the propulsion plant heat had worn away and inadvertently not been replaced. The submarine normally operated in north Atlantic waters where the sea temperature ran about thirty to forty degrees. We hadn't noticed a heat problem before.

We had lost two of the plants fairly early this trip, and while one of the problems was unrepairable so long as we remained under way, we felt we could fix the other one at sea. Of course, to work on the second machine we had to shut down three of the other air conditioning plants, and the temperature on board would climb inexorably upward. Thus, to keep the space temperatures below about ninety degrees, we would stop the repair work about every six hours and run as many plants as possible to bring the temperatures back down. Meanwhile, we were carrying out our assigned tasking: coordinating some testing with aircraft out of Bermuda.

About a week after leaving port, another air conditioning motor bit the dust. The high ship temperatures (and accompanying high humidity) were not a good environment for the motors. Unfortunately, the motor we had just lost was coupled to two air conditioning plants, so now we were down to just enough air conditioning to barely handle the heat load. Now it would take even longer to bring the temperatures down between the repair attempts. Heat makes everything tough. When you can't go anyplace to get away from the heat, it makes it hard for people even to think. It's obviously harder to work. The working area around the motors was in excess of 120°F. No luck yet with any repairs. The temperatures in the coolest spaces were rising past 100°. The propulsion plant continued to pump out heat.

Fire!

Damn. Another air conditioning motor. Maybe we can uncouple one plant and run it from another motor. Worth a try. Boy is it hot. Everyone is irritable. We seem to have dropped every wrench we have into the bilge. Everyone has stripped down to shorts and shower shoes. Dangerous to dress like that around hot metal. One of the men got a bad second-degree burn from a steam pipe while fighting the fire.

Why doesn't the commanding officer turn around and head home? This situation is almost out of control. I know he expects us to fix the problem. I wonder if we can. It's hot. Does he realize that we are not going to make it? 120° throughout the ship. I can't think. The commanding officer orders us to continue the exercise. Eight more hours go by. The temperature is still rising.

We will never make it.

I tell the commanding officer that he has to turn the ship north toward home port and declare an emergency. Surprisingly, he agrees.

I should have had the courage to brace him earlier. Now I wonder if it is not too late. We are at the end of our collective rope. I didn't appreciate how close we were to disaster. Six people slipped into coma during the first hour after we turned north. How many people will die because I didn't act earlier?

We moved the bodies to the coolest part of the boat and tried to raise medical experts on the radio. No luck. The heat and humidity in the submarine make the radio unreliable. Trying to operate the radio just adds more heat to the ship. 130°.

The weather is getting worse. A tropical storm is brewing over us. We finally get through to shore and ask for help. They will do their best, but it looks like the storm will prevent anyone from reaching us. We are on our own. The medical authorities recommend we move unconscious people to where it's cooler. Thanks.

140°. Eighteen men have lapsed into coma. Twenty-four hours since we lost our third air conditioning plant. The engineering spaces are hotter than everywhere else. I have sent all the watch-standers out of the spaces. Regulations on the minimum number of qualified people required to be present will have to be ignored. We need the crew to have some reserve in the event of a casualty. We hope this engineering plant can run itself. I am counting on it.

The storm is horrible. We are being tossed around like jacks. If we lose propulsion we will probably also lose the ship. Two other officers and I alternate as safety watches. Each of us spends five minutes in the awful heat and ten minutes out lying on the steel deck. The ship is rolling so much in the weather that we can't stay in the bunks. The temperature is so warm in the engineering spaces that I can't breathe in though my mouth. Unless I slowly drag the air in through my nose the air is much too hot for my lungs to accept. Something in the brain won't let anyone breathe in air this hot. I feel that I am slowly suffocating. Can't panic. This is undoubtedly exactly what pushed some of the men into coma.

Twenty-four men down. 145°. Forty hours since we turned and ran for help. Storm is furious above. Appears to be moving with us. No help possible from shore. Still twelve hours from port. God, I'm tired. I feel as though I am personally holding the entire ship together. If someone makes a mistake—if something more goes wrong—it will be nearly impossible to recover. It is as though we are all at the bottom of a long well, clawing at the smooth sides, trying to inch upward. A rescue ship reports that the waves are much too high to transfer our casualties. They would like to help, but cannot. We leave the "rescue ship" in our wake. We will survive or die alone.

147°. The submarine is at the mouth of the Thames River in Connecticut. Thirty-one men down. Almost home. The seawater temperature is reported as dropping below 60°. The air temperature has finally stopped rising.

Radio reports five ambulances ready on the pier. I have never been so tired in my life. None of the men in coma appear to have stopped breathing yet.

Moored. Temporary air conditioning is being supplied from the pier. The hospital says everyone who was in coma is now out of critical condition. Still serious, but all are expected to be released in the next forty-eight hours.

Glad I finally decided to demand that the commanding officer turn for home. Took me long enough to decide that it was a life-and-death situation, and our tasking was only an exercise. I am sure that some people would have died if I had kept them in the engineering spaces as the regulations required. Fortunate that three of us had the physical reserve and mental stamina to cover for the other hundred.

Wonder if we have enough fresh water on board for a shower?

*Tell them what you told them.*

Life is hard and short and the present is always important. One of the benefits of challenge and hardships is the renewed appreciation both bring to routine events. Enjoy life. Appreciate even the simple pleasures. Enjoy meeting life's challenges. Appreciate that leadership is one of the most difficult of those challenges. Leadership can truly be the difference between life and death.

Don't forget to enjoy the victories, no matter how small, that good leadership provides. Ensure that your people recognize and desire the extraordinary sweet fruits of success.

Or, in submarine talk, never miss an opportunity to take a shower.

# CHAPTER TWENTY-ONE

# Bronze

A bronze rule is a useful common tool. It is not so intrinsically valuable that it can't be bent if the situation demands. A bronze rule shouldn't be confused with a golden rule. It isn't even silver. However, decades of experience in a seawater environment have shown bronze rules resist seaworms and corrosion better than practically everything else.

Unfortunately we have discussed more than one or two ideas, which is in itself a violation of one of the rules. So this is a recapitulation of the most important concepts discussed in each chapter. Think of this chapter as a leadership three-by-five card.

## Patience

A good leader is patient. He takes every opportunity to train his subordinates and permit them to experience challenges. Leadership involves standing back and permitting young officers and executives to experience growing opportunities.

Communications skills are absolutely essential to those who aspire to leadership positions. Speaking is particularly so, and it is a learned skill. Use every opportunity to practice. Always give a brief the same attention you would a new girlfriend. Never, ever, give her a second-rate first kiss. Treat a brief the same.

# Fear

Fear is common to many professions. It also is integral to leadership. Without danger, who needs a leader? Leaders need to recognize that fear exists and take steps to ameliorate the effects, as well as compensate for the reduction in efficiency that fear produces.

Where danger is a job-related problem that must be faced, people should routinely have to deal with individual life-threatening experiences to ensure they do not forget that they can overcome fear. Through familiarity, this will also reduce the incapacitating effect of fear on large groups of inexperienced people. In many cases this can be accomplished simply by routinely exercising the unit through its full operating range.

# Winning

Winning, whether it is in sports or in an organization, results in the expectation of continued success. The stress of this expectation produces both physical and mental manifestations that can be significant burdens on decision-makers. These burdens can result in inaction. A decision not made is still a decision.

Competition in any arena teaches the individual about stress and its effects. Winning and losing frequently in competition provide the learning opportunity to compare the pain of failure to the stress of winning. Leaders are men who can persevere through the stress caused by the fear of possibly being wrong. Good leaders accept the stress of being the public person making the decisions.

# Nope

Most people and organizations are uncomfortable with decisions that are not reached by consensus, however forced and false. Preventing the achievement of consensus is thus a powerful tool to use in organizational situations when the nay-sayer does not have a position of authority.

It is possible to create situations in which a junior has supervisional responsibility for a senior. While possible, it is neither desirable nor easy. It requires continuous balancing, stroking, manipulation, and good fortune on the part of the junior. Those efforts detract from what he is able to give the organization.

If you are part of the team you share the responsibility for its failure, even if no one can draw a line of personal fault directly to your door. Men in hard jobs do not win each engagement. However, good men do not have big losses. If your organization is facing a life-and-death issue and you do not do everything in your power to stop a wrong answer, including the sacrifice of your own career, you will hold yourself responsible for any consequences.

Ensure that if and when you do place your career on the line it is over a worthwhile issue. If you have chosen such a radical move, take care that it isn't possible for your bureaucratic opponent to sidestep you and still reach his goal. Ensure you also give him every opportunity to decide not to engage.

## Growing

In your first few professional years you are soaking up experience that must last you for the rest of your life. If you are young and enjoy, or are comfortable doing, a particular job, that location probably should be caution-posted as a low-learning area.

Learning to be a leader involves getting up from your chair, going to where the action is, and getting involved. On a submarine that can be summarized as "Get up, go back, get down, and get dirty." Being a division officer is a matter of mind over sleep.

## Patterns

Humans think by a process of pattern recognition. We have difficulty thinking when there are too many small things wrong or a major discrepancy in the pattern.

Good leaders eliminate distractions and impediments to pattern recognition—they eliminate the dirt, debris and abnormal conditions from the work place. Good leaders build situations in which both patterns and pattern breaks are obvious.

## Change

People are comfortable with continuity and patterns. Thus, we have difficulty recognizing when there is a need for change, and we also have trouble adapting to change. We often underestimate its significance. Those people who can recognize the need for change and identify the specific change necessary are of extraordinary value to the organization.

A facilitator to recognizing the need for change is a continuous reevaluation of whether the organization's efforts make sense in the light of current goals. Another facilitator is being sensitive to "bumps" in a profession that are too minor to cause problems. Don't let a bump go unnoticed or unmarked. There is always a dirty reason coiled underneath.

## Admission

When you find something you enjoy doing, don't let the job's inevitable little detractions and distractions get you down. With time you can always fix them. All you have to do is make it near the top.

There is always a price of admission.

## Assignments

The most important policies in any large organization concern how and where people are assigned. The overriding consideration is the needs of the organization. The quality of the force is higher if the better people are assigned to the tougher jobs. One should not worry about rewarding good performers with easy follow-on tours. They don't have time for easy tours. Success is its own reward for true achievers.

People are unable to look above them in the organization and determine the job that is best for them. Permitting them to choose assignments is therefore an unwise policy. In any bureaucratic organization the jobs change faster than the job descriptions are altered. Campaigning for your next job is asking for the chance to place your round body in a square hole.

People should be moved frequently in an organization. The unit's natural chauvinistic resistance to "new guys" serves to screen and unmask wrong facts and bad ideas. Moving people between units in the organization makes it easier to generate and spread new ideas. At the same time it becomes easier to overcome small-group resistance to higher standards and goals.

People should also never be retoured in the same unit. Staying in the same unit, even in a different job, reduces the learning pace and the level of expertise that will be reached.

# Limits

When problems are reported, investigate every one. Keep your perspective; the smoke may be in the mind of the beholder.

If you want to find out your problems before your boss does, don't kill the messenger and never, never intimidate to hold down the noise.

Listen to everyone, particularly people you don't like and people with whom you don't agree. People who are not fond of you may provide the most accurate reflection of the effects of your policies. If you don't keep an unfriend around, visit one more frequently than you do your dentist.

The organization reflects society. If there is a part of society that it is important your people not mirror, you have to pay a special price to establish and maintain the right conditions.

The image your organization projects is important. If you do not like that image, the solution is not public relations, but changing reality until it gives the image you want.

The organization's most limited resources are good people and money. Solving a problem without investing either is possible, but leadership and hard work have their limits. Make sure you can afford a cheap decision.

# One-Two

As long as a leader can reduce what he wants the organization to achieve to a number of goals no higher than the number of wishes Aladdin had, the leader will also have the opportunity to achieve truly magical results.

Any leader can demand and get from his people one or two extraordinary achievements. The more difficult part is conceiving and framing goals that truly make a difference, and then supervising to prevent the organization from wasting its assets wandering down fruitless trails.

## Up Or

People are your organization's most important asset. Don't forget it when times get tough. Good organizations are always making their best efforts to attract, recruit, sort, and keep good people. Don't forget it takes money as well as leadership. The good people leave first. They can easily find new jobs. It is the deadwood that stays with you.

## Egregious

Organizations that want warriors face two critical problems in peacetime. The first is how to avoid selecting the sheep who looks good, causes the minimum problems, and is at the same time incapable of the decisiveness and risk-taking that are imperative in wartime. The second problem is how to identify the good leader who has made it past the initial screening process in which he was closely monitored and subsequently develops a problem, such as alcoholism, that affects his judgment.

Identifying the alcoholic is hard. The commander receives little help from the individual or his family because they hide and protect him. The same is true of the people with whom the alcoholic works, even though such behavior is normally not in their best interests. The leader also receives little assistance from "social" units, for the natural reason that their priorities are with the individual first, whereas the leader usually places the organization first. Identifying the alcoholic is a tough command decision.

## Voting

One bad leader is a malignant cancer in an organization. His faults are hidden or disguised when his seniors are present and therefore are often invisible to them, but they are obvious to those in the organization who are junior to him, lingering everywhere like the malodorous smell of a pulp mill.

In the submarine force the most reliable and direct evidence of poor command leadership is a low rate of retention of junior officers. Unhappy people vote with their feet.

# Walking

Management by walking around prevents the executive from being captured by his staff or inefficient subordinates. Getting out and around provides the leader with raw inputs for evaluation and gets his experience into the field. Walking around increases the possibility that the executive will get to hear or see some of the hard problems that exist in the organization. Walking is great anticapture insurance.

Paper management systems provide an excuse for not walking around the organization. No paper system is as good as a pair of comfortable shoes.

Walking away from your executives and letting them work results in more originality, permits you to coordinate a larger span of control, and gives you the opportunity to look at harder problems that require judgment or abstract conceptualization.

If you have a boss and want to increase the scope of operational freedom you are granted, operate your organization so it is accessible and open to both your boss and his staff. This system will also provide you more access to your supervisor's staff.

# Integrity

Truth sells itself. Truth gets you through situations nothing else will.

Looking dumb is oodles better than lying.

The risk of false accusation is one of those risks that accompany success and senior leadership positions. The only way to insure yourself against this risk is to be publicly, privately, and deliberately squeaky clean.

Integrity ensures you solve and do not ignore real problems. It acts as a forcing function for needed improvements.

Lack of integrity on the part of an individual is often a key indicator of a deeper problem in the organization or unit.

Integrity is the only product Congress or the Pentagon is interested in buying from a professional warrior.

## Location

Weak leaders never find themselves where action unexpectedly breaks out. They are always supervising somewhere else.

If you intend to take chances, put your own body up front. You tend to stop dangerous actions sooner the closer your own body is to the action end of the order chain. You'll hurt fewer people in the long run.

Bravery is a learned skill. If you are in the leadership business you are in the business of not letting your body react naturally to fear. Seize every opportunity to put yourself where the danger is most intense—where if you don't slay the dragon, the dragon eats you. Learn through experience how close you can stand to the dragon's breath and still control your emotions.

## Communicating

The chain of command is valuable bureaucratic protection for juniors. If the chain of command is being bypassed it is because the chain of command is not adding value.

The supervisor in an organization does not believe in "good" surprises.

The supervisor's belief in his junior's personal loyalty is critical to a satisfactory working relationship. The junior must earn that belief and keep it.

Weekly reviews of what has been done, learned, and planned, and how those things have or will help or affect the supervisor, are spaced at about the right frequency. Daily reports are usually too frequent, even for the straw that stirs the drink.

Routine, periodic written self-reviews are valuable. Logical missteps are more difficult to miss in black-and-white assessments.

# Bullets

To recover from a mistake the individual needs to know what happened, why it was serious, and what changes have to be made. There are no leadership mistakes attributable to acts of God.

Successfully disagreeing with a senior is always difficult. Successfully disagreeing in public is a hundred times harder.

A good leader does not routinely operate at more than eighty percent of his physical and emotional capacity.

# Opportunities

Life is short. Challenges ignored or sidestepped are opportunities that never occur again.

It is a mistake to live in the future. The future is much too uncertain. The moment is now. Change what you can't control.

Enjoy life. Enjoy the victories a full life gives, no matter how small. Never miss the opportunity to take a shower.

# Silver

Treat everyone with respect. Think about the effects of your words and actions on others.